FLASH POINTS

FLASH
POINTS

Igniting the Hidden Passions of Your Soul

STEPHEN
ARTERBURN

with Angela Hunt

TYNDALE HOUSE PUBLISHERS, INC.
WHEATON, ILLINOIS

Visit Tyndale's exciting Web site at www.tyndale.com

Flashpoints

Copyright © 2002 by Stephen Arterburn. All rights reserved. Written permission must be secured from the publisher to use or reproduce any part of this book, except for brief quotations in critical reviews or articles.

Cover photograph © 2001 by Terry Vine/Getty Images. All rights reserved.

Interior and back cover photograph by Julie Chen, © 2001 by Tyndale House Publishers, Inc.

Interior and back cover photograph of Stephen Arterburn © 2001 by David Riley Associates. All rights reserved.

Designed by Julie Chen

Edited by Dave Lindstedt

Published in association with the literary agency of Alive Communications, Inc., 7680 Goddard Street, Suite 200, Colorado Springs, CO 80920

Unless otherwise indicated, all Scripture quotations are taken from the *Holy Bible*, New Living Translation, copyright © 1996. Used by permission of Tyndale House Publishers, Inc., Wheaton, Illinois 60189. All rights reserved.

Scripture quotations marked NASB are taken from the *New American Standard Bible*, © 1960, 1962, 1963, 1968, 1971, 1972, 1973, 1975, 1977 by The Lockman Foundation. Used by permission.

Some details in the anecdotal stories used in this book have been altered slightly to preserve the privacy of the individuals involved.

Library of Congress Cataloging-in-Publication Data

Arterburn, Stephen, date.
 Flashpoints : igniting the hidden passions of your soul / Stephen Arterburn with Angela Hunt.
  p. cm.
Includes bibliographical references.
 ISBN 0-8423-5753-X (alk. paper)—ISBN 0-8423-5754-8 (pbk.)
 1. Christian life. 2. Change—Religious aspects—Christianity. I. Hunt, Angela Elwell, date.
 II. Title.
BV4509.5 .A76 2002
248.4—dc21   2001007368

Printed in the United States of America

08 07 06 05 04 03 02
 8   7   6   5   4   3   2

MY DEEPEST APPRECIATION to Ron Beers, who called me one day and asked me what I thought about an inspirational book on the turning points that change everything in people's lives.

I owe a tremendous debt to Angela Hunt, who turned this dream and my challenged writing into a book. Angela, when I read *The Note,* your incredible novel, I never dreamed I would have the honor of writing a book with you. Thanks for sharing your talent with me.

Finally, thanks to Greg Johnson, one of those rare, brilliant people who know what they are doing and do it so well. Thanks for directing me and challenging me as a writer and as a person. You are the dream agent of all agents.

"CHANGE
IS NOT MERELY

NECESSARY TO LIFE,
"IT *IS* LIFE."

—ALVIN TOFFLER

CONTENTS

FINDING YOUR FLASHPOINT

SOMEONE ONCE ASKED Jean Cocteau, the French writer, artist, and film director, what he would take if his house were on fire and he could remove only one thing. He replied, "I would take the fire."

"I would take the fire."

In one sense, Cocteau's answer seems an obvious, almost practical solution. Take the fire from a burning building, and the building will no longer burn. But I think he may have meant it in another way. As a writer and an artist, he knew that fire—*passion*—is an indispensable ingredient in the creative process. And if he could have only one thing, he would take the fire every time.

Passion—that fire in the belly—is the catalyst of every vibrant life, whether it's lived in Paris, France, or in Small-town, USA. It's as vital to the young mother at home as it is to the corporate executive. The fire of passion can change a life, and one passionate life can change the world.

THE IRRESISTIBLE FORCE OF FIRE

Any firefighter will tell you that fire is predictably unpredictable. Under the right circumstances even a small fire can pose a great danger. If a blaze reaches the flash point, sometimes called the flashover temperature, every bit of combustible material in the room—wood, paper, carpet, drapes, and furniture—will explode into flame. The fire doesn't even have to touch anything in order to spread. A confined blaze will heat the atmosphere in the room until *everything* in the enclosed space spontaneously ignites. If it can burn, at the flash point it will.

If we apply the same principle to the world of ideas, the result is equally explosive. When dormant passions burst into flame, and ideas spontaneously ignite, everything within our circle of influence will be changed forever. As frightening and dangerous as a fiery flash point can be, a "flashpoint" of the heart can set the world on fire!

Has this ever happened to you? A small fire—a dream, a hope, a desire—smoldering quietly within the confines of your heart, begins to edge toward the flashover temperature. You begin to feel the heat, and as your passion grows, so does your inspiration, motivation, and determination. Suddenly, status quo is no longer satisfactory. You must take action. You won't be content until the flame of your spirit kindles a wildfire in your soul, transforming your life and the lives of others. The flashpoint occurs when you are compelled to make a change—or make a difference—no matter what the cost.

Some of us, however, are like the sprinkler system in an office building. At the first sign of heat or smoke (natural by-products of every hot new idea), we've conditioned ourselves to spray cold water on even the barest flame of desire. Maybe that was how we were raised. Or maybe it's just plain fear. But it doesn't have to be that way.

If you have had a flashpoint experience, you know how it has changed your perspective. If you have not yet experienced a flashpoint and its revolutionary aftereffects, you can—and you *will*—by simply opening your eyes to the opportunities around you. If you refuse—if you choose to stay stuck right where you are, you may miss the fullness of life that God intended for you.

In the movie *The Sixth Sense,* a little boy with unusual powers looks up at the character played by Bruce Willis and says, "I see dead people." As I look at the world around me, I have something in common with that little boy. I see dead people, too, but they're still walking around in the flesh. Their eyes reflect the sorry truth that their soul has become shriveled and dry and desperate. They've lost their purpose and reason for living—or they've never found it. Their lives are a grind, and they feel victimized by everyone and everything. Their deadness is emotional and spiritual rather than physical, but they are no less dead. The good news is they don't have to *stay* that way.

If I've just described your life, this book may be the spark that leads to a life-changing flashpoint. I pray that it is.

A DINNER THAT CRYSTALLIZED MY OUTLOOK

Several years ago, I was privileged to be among a group invited to a dinner with former president Gerald Ford and former Soviet president Mikhail Gorbachev. (I know, I know—Billy Graham and Mother Teresa both told me I shouldn't name-drop.) President Ford arrived first, and with genuine warmth and a statesman's air, he walked to each person in the room, greeted him or her with a smile and a handshake, then stepped back to await Mr. Gorbachev's arrival.

I happened to be standing near the entrance when Mr. Gorbachev's bodyguard opened the double doors. The Russian statesman walked straight toward me, shook my hand, and through his interpreter said it was good to see me. He asked if we had met before, remarking that I looked familiar. I assured him that this was our first meeting because I would never have forgotten the privilege.

As we settled into our seats, I was struck by the friendliness of both Mr. Gorbachev and President Ford, especially in contrast to the chilly self-importance of another dignitary, a prominent minister, who had also been invited. Unlike the two national leaders, this man greeted no one but the guests of honor. The rest of us seemed invisible.

As the evening proceeded, I was inspired and awed by the sense of watching history unfold in the presence of these two great men. I later realized that both Gorbachev and Ford had had flashpoint experiences that had not only changed their own lives but the course of history.

Gerald Ford's flashpoint came when he pardoned Richard Nixon, a difficult and controversial decision that probably cost him the 1976 election. Remarkably, he made the decision despite the personal consequences. Only recently have historians begun to recognize Ford's courage in pardoning Nixon. The impeachment proceedings involving President Bill Clinton showed how the nation might have been distracted from more important issues had Nixon been prosecuted after leaving office. Gerald Ford's steadfast wisdom was needed at that moment in history, and he sacrificed himself to act on his convictions.

Likewise, when Mikhail Gorbachev's flashpoint moment arrived, he was willing to sacrifice his personal interests for the sake of his country. By then he had already established himself as a man of high standards and principles. For example, when he was in college, he and his family had very little money. For clothing he had only one suit, one tie, and one white dress shirt. But he would not allow himself to look shabby among his classmates. Every day for four years he cleaned that one outfit and pressed his one shirt so he would be as well dressed as his peers.

At the dinner, Gorbachev spoke of the moment he realized that communism could not and should not endure. As he had risen in office, he gained greater access to data about the Soviet Union's strengths and weaknesses. In studying this information, he became increasingly aware that he and the Russian people were victims of a great deception, and he was stunned when he learned that the USSR was financially unstable and had few resources for economic correction. Although at first he was unwilling to admit the truth, he began to see that the system he had believed in and lived for was a sham. He knew it could not survive, and he began to believe that it *should* not survive. He explained that he finally realized that all he had been taught was false, and from that moment on he felt compelled to expose the lies of past communist leaders. Although the Russian people have suffered through severe financial difficulties in the transition between communism and democracy, they have moved toward a better way of life since Gorbachev's change of heart. And as a further result of Gorbachev's flashpoint, the cold war ended, the Berlin Wall came down, and the political affairs of the world were forever altered.

As I reflected on that evening and my encounters with those two statesmen, I realized how powerful and world-changing an individual flashpoint could be.

FLASHPOINTS ARE NOT GENDER SPECIFIC

Men don't hold the franchise on flashpoints. Plenty of women around the world have changed and influenced the lives of others through their own life-changing flashpoint experiences.

Princess Diana, weary of living in a glass palace, took royalty to the streets and to the hospital beds of suffering children. She could have remained cloistered in the comfort of her royal life of luxury, but she saw an opportunity to express the fullness of her heart and responded. And though her life was cut short, she made a difference.

Mother Teresa could have chosen the sterile halls of any hospital in the world, but instead she chose the filthy streets of Calcutta, India, where the sick and the dying lie in the gutters like discarded bags of trash. Along with the Sisters of Mercy, she made it her mission to ensure that the poor of Calcutta would at least die with dignity.

Rosa Parks changed the course of our nation when she refused to move to the back of the bus. In a flashpoint of insight, anger, and persistence, she ignited a firestorm of change that still burns brightly in our society today. Her steadfast resistance to prejudice and inequality became a rallying point for those who sought to bring equal protection and fairness under the law to people of all races.

In 1987, Georgia Nucci received word that her only daughter, Jennifer, an exchange student in Ecuador, had contracted hepatitis. By the time Georgia and her husband arrived in Ecuador to care for their daughter, Jennifer was in a coma. A few days later, she died.

A few months after the grieving parents returned home to Claverack, New York, their nineteen-year-old son, Christopher, left for England to spend a semester abroad in a Syracuse University overseas program. Returning home on December 21, 1988, he boarded Pan Am Flight 103 and died when a terrorist bomb destroyed the plane over Lockerbie, Scotland.

"For about a month after each child died," Georgia told *Parade* magazine, "it was as if I had had major surgery. I felt physically battered. That kind of grief is very physical. I hurt as if there was a trail of blood behind me."

Georgia set about doing things to ease the terrible burden of grief she bore. She helped the other stricken parents of Flight 103 by collecting stories and compiling scrapbooks. She lobbied the aviation industry to provide more accurate records and passenger manifests. But despite her busyness, a hole remained in her heart. "As a consequence of terrorism, I was no longer a mother," she said. "I wanted to regain my status as a mother. Terrorism wasn't going to have another victim in me. On Christopher's birthday, in March 1990, we decided we wanted to adopt a child."

Because most U.S. orphanages considered the Nuccis too old (at the time, Georgia was forty-seven and Tony forty-nine), they investigated foreign adoption and learned that up to 40,000 children are abandoned every day around the world. When they saw a picture of four siblings from Colombia, ages two to ten, who had been abandoned by their mother because she could no longer care for them, their hearts told them what they had to do. They brought the children home, struggled through all the necessary adjustments, and began the serious work of creating a family.

"I suppose I could have sat in the corner and sucked my thumb for eternity," Georgia said. But she didn't. After the children had adjusted to their new home, Georgia enrolled in law school, at age fifty-one. Today she is a staff attorney for the New York Department of Taxation and Finance. "My life," she said, "is fuller than it's ever been."[1]

Her flashpoint, born of grief, brought love and hope back into the lives of four children—and untold numbers of people who will benefit from her efforts to heal the grief caused by terrorism.

HAVE YOU FELT THE INNER SPARK?

Gerald Ford, Mikhail Gorbachev, Princess Diana, Mother Teresa, Rosa Parks, Georgia Nucci. In their own way, each of these people came to a flashpoint and made a courageous decision, one that impacted many lives beyond their own. Has your life been transformed by a flashpoint experience? Did it follow a frustrating struggle to succeed or a failure to conquer? Did it come in the aftershocks of tragedy, the loss of someone you loved, or the destruction of something you valued? Perhaps you reached your flashpoint after achieving a pinnacle of success, only to find it unfulfilling. Or maybe it was a startling moment of insight when you caught a glimpse of how life could be if only you would choose to live differently.

Some people never reach their flashpoint. Instead, they

soldier on, living what Henry David Thoreau called "lives of quiet desperation," filled with regrets and dead dreams. Undoubtedly you know men and women who willingly "stay the course" through loneliness, despair, and self-destruction. They persist in old patterns and habits because they believe life can't get any better and that everyone suffers to some degree without hope. The leg irons of predictability and routine bind them to their desperate lifestyle.

This book is about unshackling ourselves from the past and stepping out of our self-imposed prisons. It's about trading our mundane existence for exuberant life; exchanging the predictable routine for amazing feats, thrills, surprises, and delights. When we surrender our hopelessness and grasp onto new opportunities, we'll discover a new way to live, awaken our dormant talents, and inspire others by our shining example.

Do you believe it? Do you have a dream you're afraid to follow? Perhaps life has dropped you into a difficult situation you didn't choose. Perhaps you are tired of living in quiet desperation and long for the freedom to break out. Perhaps you yearn to get your high school diploma, lose fifty pounds, or find the courage to escape an abusive situation. I don't know what you're facing, but I do know that you can come to a flashpoint and make a decision about finding or making a better life. You can follow in the footsteps of those who have transformed their lives and changed the world for all of us.

Dreamers can be found in every bed, but the adventurers are those who wake up and refuse to leave their dreams behind. When we muster the courage to act on our dreams, the ensuing flashpoints will lead to new opportunities for ourselves, our loved ones, our friends and neighbors—and sometimes for the entire world.

If you've been slumbering beneath the covers, filled with what-ifs and why-nots, perhaps it is time to stop dreaming and wake up to the possibilities that flood your life. Get up. Get out into the world and make a difference. Today is a great day for positive change!

MY FLASHPOINT

I have experienced several flashpoints in my life (yes, you can have more than one!), but let me tell you about the one making the most difference in my life today.

In 1995, with my eyes and heart open to new ideas, I attended my first Peter Lowe Success Seminar. The event, held in the Anaheim Pond, featured great speakers like Zig Ziglar, Robert Schuller, Larry King, and a host of others. The mood was exciting, the atmosphere intense, and even though today I can't recall a single specific quote from any of the speakers, they had a tremendous impact. Something that day, whatever it was, touched a place that had been stirring within me for years. As the speakers interacted with the crowd, I began to observe the audience. The Anaheim arena has about 18,000 seats, and on this particular day 7,000 people had taken time from work to come hear these motivational speakers.

Then it happened. In an instant my mind filled with a dazzling idea, a vision that still amazes me to this day. I looked around and said to myself, *No one has ever brought the finest Christian female communicators together in one place like this. If I could coordinate that kind of event, we could fill every seat, not neces-*

*sarily to motivate women for "success," but simply to encourage them.
I believe they need it—and they deserve it.*

I returned to my office the next day and called Barbara
Johnson, a woman I had met years before. She happens to be
the best-selling Christian female author of all time, with books
like *Where Does a Mother Go to Resign?* and *Stick a Geranium in
Your Hat and Be Happy.* If calling her sounds like a big step
(and it was!), remember that a flashpoint brings with it the
inspiration and motivation to take action. When Barbara
answered the phone, I told her my idea and asked if she would
like to be a part of it. Amazingly, she said yes.

Emboldened, I then called Patsy Clairmont, another best-
selling Christian author, whom I had met at a dinner given by
the publishing division of Focus on the Family. At the dinner,
while everyone clamored for Dr. Dobson's attention, I noticed
a small woman sitting with her husband over in the corner.
Thinking they might want some company, I walked over to
visit. Only later did I discover that Patsy was the keynote
speaker for the evening! When her turn came, she stood on
a chair (she's tiny!) and soon had that crowd wrapped around
her little finger.

Patsy and I had spoken several times since that night, and
when I called to discuss the possibility of a women's conference, she said she'd sign on if I persevered. These commit-
ments from two hugely successful authors proved to be the
defining answers to my plan. I went on to contact Marilyn
Meberg and Luci Swindoll, and soon we had formed a team.
We cleared the dates for six events in 1996 and began to
promote them.

We held the first conference at a church in southern

California. Before the first speaker stepped to the podium, all 2,300 seats were filled. An additional three hundred women watched on live television in an overflow room. The great response of the women to the speakers led to many changed lives. I knew we were on to something, so we began to expand the vision.

During the first year, 30,000 women attended our events. We hosted 150,000 the second year. The third year's conference attracted 300,000 women, and now we average more than 300,000 each year. Our vision has become known as Women of Faith, and it is the largest conference event in America, visiting nearly thirty cities a year with a message of encouragement and hope for women. Women of Faith, which began as a tiny flashpoint, became a pinnacle in my life.

What makes the success of Women of Faith even more amazing to me is the failure that preceded it. The year before I attended the Peter Lowe conference, I had coordinated a twelve-city tour called "Winning at Work Without Losing at Love" with myself as the featured speaker. The total turnout for that less-than-stellar event—adding up the audience from all twelve cities—was just over one thousand people. In Chicago, we drew a grand total of thirty-six attendees, at least ten of whom came from clinics I operated in the area. I felt like one big loser going around talking about winning.

But even though the star attraction—yours truly—failed to attract much attention, that speaking tour wasn't a total loss. Through it I learned how to produce and promote a traveling seminar. As humbling as it was at the time, I can see now how God used that experience as a training ground for Women of Faith. In 1997, we held a Women of Faith conference at the

Anaheim Pond, the same place where I had experienced my flashpoint. This time, every single seat was filled.

I am often asked why I think God chose me, a man, to begin Women of Faith. I don't fully know the answer to that question, but I do know that God can put the pieces of our life together like a jigsaw puzzle—the good, the bad, and the ugly—to make a beautiful picture. In my case, for years I had seen women as objects and treated them disdain-fully. Over time, as God touched and healed some deep wounds in my life, my view of women began to change. Out of that healing came a desire to give something back to women, to atone for what I had taken. My flashpoint moment may have occurred in 1995, but my desire to minis-ter to women had come as a revelation years earlier. Since the beginning of Women of Faith, sparks from that single flash-point have resulted in the burning embers of grace, love, and joy igniting salvation in the hearts of more than 1.5 million women.

I have to be honest. I've made some big mistakes in my life. But I've learned that it's never too late to change. It's never too late to find the life you desire. All it takes is one flashpoint and one decision to fire your passions and move you toward your dreams.

"But I don't have time to change! I barely have time to read this book!"

I hear that cry. If your life is full of rushing from one thing to another, it's time to stop and take stock of the situation. Friend, you don't have time to continue living in a mad rush. What is life, if not the investment of time? Mark this: If you are not spending your days and hours in a way that satisfies and thrills your soul, it's time for some internal combustion. Let your dreams, desires, and passions build to a flashpoint and set your soul on fire. Decide right now to live differently from this moment forward.

If you're ready to read the next page, you're ready for a flashpoint. My task is to show you how simple it can be to change from merely existing to living a passionate life. Sound far-fetched? As Walt Disney used to say, "It's kind of fun to do the impossible!"[2]

2

SPIRITUAL FLASHPOINTS

LET'S TAKE A LOOK at a flashpoint—a fictional one, but one that illustrates a very real decision that each of us must make. We might even call this the ultimate flashpoint. In *The Silver Chair* by C. S. Lewis, a young girl named Jill, who is quite thirsty, discovers a stream—but also finds it guarded by a lion.

> "Are you not thirsty?" said the Lion.
>
> "I'm *dying* of thirst," said Jill.
>
> "Then drink," said the Lion.
>
> "May I—could I—would you mind going away while I do?" said Jill.
>
> The Lion answered this only by a look and a very low growl. And as Jill gazed at its motionless bulk, she realized that she might as well have asked the whole mountain to move aside for her convenience. . . .
>
> "Will you promise not to—do anything to me, if I do come?" said Jill.

"I make no promise," said the Lion.

Jill was so thirsty now that, without noticing it, she had come a step nearer.

"Do you eat girls?" she asked.

"I have swallowed up girls and boys, women and men, kings and emperors, cities and realms," said the Lion. It didn't say this as if it were boasting, nor as if it were sorry, nor as if it were angry. It just said it.

"I daren't come and drink," said Jill.

"Then you will die of thirst," said the Lion.

"Oh dear!" said Jill, coming another step nearer. "I suppose I must go and look for another stream then."

"There is no other stream," said the Lion.[1]

In this allegory, part of Lewis's Chronicles of Narnia series, Aslan the Lion represents Jesus Christ, the Lion of Judah. During his time on earth, Jesus himself said, "I am the way, the truth, and the life. No one can come to the Father except through me" (John 14:6). If you are thirsty, if you long for a purpose in life and a sense of belonging, come to Jesus.

In the all-important flashpoint moment that leads to salvation, each of us must come to the place where we see ourselves as God sees us, and we realize we need Christ because nothing we could ever do would be enough to earn God's grace and goodness. When we make the decision to surrender our life, we come away from that flashpoint with a new purpose—to live for Christ. We don't always know quite how that's going to work, but we accept by faith that Christ and Christ alone will satisfy our soul's deepest need.

In Mark 8:36-37, Jesus asks two penetrating questions: "And how do you benefit if you gain the whole world but lose your own soul in the process? Is anything worth more than your soul?" If you haven't yet made this all-important flashpoint decision, may I invite you to do it now? Apart from new life in Christ, no other flashpoint has enduring value.

FLASHPOINT: MEETING OUR WILD AND POWERFUL SAVIOR

A spiritual flashpoint can be a frightening experience—at least it will be if we understand the power and majesty of our Creator. Once more, C. S. Lewis, in *The Lion, the Witch, and the Wardrobe,* illustrates the respectful fear that would accompany an encounter with the living God:[2]

> "Is—is he a man?" asked Lucy.
>
> "Aslan a man!" said Mr. Beaver sternly.
> "Certainly not. . . . Don't you know who is the King of Beasts? Aslan is a lion—*the* Lion, the great Lion."
>
> "Ooh!" said Susan. "I'd thought he was a man. Is he—quite safe? I shall feel rather nervous about meeting a lion."
>
> "That you will, dearie, and no mistake," said Mrs. Beaver; "if there's anyone who can appear before Aslan without their knees knocking, they're either braver than most or else just silly."
>
> "Then he isn't safe?" said Lucy.
>
> "Safe?" said Mr. Beaver; "don't you hear what Mrs. Beaver tells you? Who said anything about safe?

'Course he isn't safe. But he's good. He's the King,
I tell you."[3]

God is good, but he is not safe, and he is not ours to control.
He is bigger than we are and infinitely more powerful, more
wrathful, more holy than we could ever hope to be. But he
is good, and he is love. And he expresses that love to us in
a thousand intimate, gentle ways. Those who reject his love
stand in danger of his wrath, but those who accept his love,
coupled with his power and authority, are drawn close in a
comforting embrace.

Cleansed from our sins and fired by the Spirit with holy
enthusiasm, we set out to walk in a new life—only to get
sidetracked. Although our salvation is settled in heaven,
sometimes we become confused about *how* we should be
living. And that's when we often have other spiritual
flashpoints—when our loving Lord reveals more of himself,
his plan, or his mercy.

Too often people believe that once they accept Christ, all
the issues of life ought to easily and magically fall into place.
Some even try to use their salvation as an excuse not to
change, get help, or grow. But none of us ever arrives at a
point where we are exempt from the need to change. We
need to be willing to grow when a flashpoint of insight comes
to mind—even those times when the flashpoint hurts.

FLASHPOINT:
GROWTH CAN BE PAINFUL

A few years ago, my wife and I experienced a bad spot in our
marriage. Over time we had grown more and more irritated

with each other. We still slept in the same bed, but the distance between our hearts was like a chasm.

When Sandy could no longer stand the chilly atmosphere in our home, she asked me to live somewhere else. In that flashpoint moment, I saw that my "being right" was less important than our being together. We never separated, but the next time we met was in a counselor's office. After a thought-provoking session with a very skillful female therapist, I realized that I needed to do whatever it took to keep my marriage together. I had made a commitment on our wedding day to meet Sandy's needs, no matter what the price, right or wrong, justified or not. My flashpoint was a painful experience, but it led to healing and the restoration of my relationship with my wife.

You may be facing a problem so large, so looming, that you can't even imagine a life without fear, dread, and worry. If so, you may need to look inward to discover what is confining you and preventing your release to a hopeful future. What binds you? A dreadful past? Food? Alcohol? Self-pity?

Are you bound by an inappropriate relationship? abuse? a phobia? Whatever it is, choose to make this day a flashpoint that will begin the process of changing your life for good, forever.

Not long ago I received the following e-mail from a man who had experienced a spiritual flashpoint after reading something I had written:

> Thank you for the book *Every Man's Battle;*[4] it is a godsend. I have been battling pornography for about nine months now, and it has been spiritually draining. I always figured prayer would be enough, but after

many broken promises to God and myself, I was feeling defeated and didn't know what to do.

Thank you for addressing the need to tame my
eyes. I have been making a covenant with my eyes
for about a week now, though it's not easy. It seems
to be becoming second nature; now when I start to
look at a woman in an inappropriate way I tell myself
she is God's creation, and I pray for him to let me see
her through his eyes. This has been a hard struggle as
a single man who has tasted of the fruit of marriage.
I was married for four years, but my wife left though
I wanted repentance and restoration.

First were R-rated movies, then occasionally
porn, but as you know the guilt is more than I
bargained for. Now I choose obedience, not mere
excellence. Thank you for the straightforward truth.

Others who struggle with lust have to come to similar significant flashpoints. I have worked with men who were obsessed
with a woman or burned with desire for another man. When
I asked them about these dangerously inappropriate obsessions,
they usually said something like, "I have asked God to take
this from me."

If you identify with that statement, let me challenge you to
go beyond it. Stop waiting for God to do what God is waiting
for *you* to do. God doesn't want your comfort to increase; he
wants your character to grow! Rather than ask him to function as your push-button, quick-fix, instant relief provider, be
obedient and rid your life of sin. Follow his instructions. A
quick fix would be nice, but you wouldn't learn anything
from it.

Temptation is the desire to fulfill a natural yearning in an inappropriate way. When we are in the throes of temptation, burning with desire for something to which we are not entitled, God intends for us to do something: Run! God's solution is quite simple. In the words of Solomon, "My child, if sinners entice you, turn your back on them!" (Proverbs 1:10).

In counseling Timothy, his young protégé, the apostle Paul wrote:

> RUN FROM ANYTHING THAT STIMULATES YOUTHFUL LUST.
> FOLLOW ANYTHING THAT MAKES YOU WANT TO DO RIGHT.
> PURSUE FAITH AND LOVE AND PEACE, AND ENJOY THE COMPANIONSHIP OF THOSE WHO CALL ON THE LORD WITH PURE HEARTS.
>
> 2 TIMOTHY 2:22

God says to flee temptation. He also says that temptation comes from inside us. So rather than asking God to fix it, *you* need to fix it. Run, by not looking and lusting after that person. Run, by replacing lust for someone else with love for your spouse. Run, by moving toward the help you need to build character. Run, by connecting with people who can help heal your soul.

If you do whatever it takes to resolve your lust—or whatever it is you struggle against, God will begin to remove the temptation. He will bless your efforts, for your sake and for the sake of those you love.

According to James, when you flee those things that are inappropriate, you build up your endurance and your character:

21

> DEAR BROTHERS AND SISTERS, WHENEVER TROUBLE [TEMPTATION]
> COMES YOUR WAY, LET IT BE AN OPPORTUNITY FOR JOY. FOR
> WHEN YOUR FAITH IS TESTED, YOUR ENDURANCE HAS A CHANCE
> TO GROW. SO LET IT GROW, FOR WHEN YOUR ENDURANCE IS
> FULLY DEVELOPED, YOU WILL BE STRONG IN CHARACTER AND
> READY FOR ANYTHING.   JAMES 1:2-4

In a spiritual flashpoint, we learn to focus on the needs of
others instead of obsessing over our own desires. The spiritual
life is about surrender instead of control, and repentance rather
than obstinacy.

FLASHPOINT: A BURNING BUSH IN THE DESERT

You may be familiar with the story of Moses. Exiled for forty
years in the land of Midian after he fled from Egypt, where his
compatriots, the children of Israel, lived as slaves, Moses had a
flashpoint experience when he noticed a burning bush in the
desert:

> ONE DAY MOSES WAS TENDING THE FLOCK OF HIS FATHER-IN-
> LAW, JETHRO, THE PRIEST OF MIDIAN, AND HE WENT DEEP INTO
> THE WILDERNESS NEAR SINAI, THE MOUNTAIN OF GOD.
> SUDDENLY, THE ANGEL OF THE LORD APPEARED TO HIM AS A
> BLAZING FIRE IN A BUSH. MOSES WAS AMAZED BECAUSE THE BUSH
> WAS ENGULFED IN FLAMES, BUT IT DIDN'T BURN UP. "AMAZING!"
> MOSES SAID TO HIMSELF. "WHY ISN'T THAT BUSH BURNING UP?
> I MUST GO OVER TO SEE THIS."

WHEN THE LORD SAW THAT HE HAD CAUGHT MOSES' ATTEN-
TION, GOD CALLED TO HIM FROM THE BUSH, "MOSES! MOSES!"

"HERE I AM!" MOSES REPLIED.

"DO NOT COME ANY CLOSER," GOD TOLD HIM. "TAKE OFF
YOUR SANDALS, FOR YOU ARE STANDING ON HOLY GROUND."

THEN HE SAID, "I AM THE GOD OF YOUR ANCESTORS—THE GOD
OF ABRAHAM, THE GOD OF ISAAC, AND THE GOD OF JACOB."

WHEN MOSES HEARD THIS, HE HID HIS FACE IN HIS HANDS
BECAUSE HE WAS AFRAID TO LOOK AT GOD.   EXODUS 3:1-6

Can you imagine how Moses must have felt? Out of simple
curiosity, he had walked over to examine a blazing thornbush—
and found himself face-to-face with *the angel of the Lord,* the
Old Testament term for Jesus Christ, the physical manifesta-
tion of God. Not only that, but God called his name—twice, for
emphasis.

It could happen to you. In the heat of a thorny situation,
through the most unlikely circumstances, or perhaps in the
middle of just another day of tending the sheep, God will
manifest himself and call your name. He will communicate
with you—just as he spoke to Moses—in a way that you can
understand. Sometimes he whispers in a still, small voice; other
times he speaks through an inner urging; but when God calls
your name, you will know it. And whether it's by the desperation of your circumstances or simple curiosity, you'll be
compelled to respond.

When Moses realized that someone unusual was calling his
name, he no doubt braced himself for a most unusual conversation!

> THEN THE LORD TOLD HIM, "YOU CAN BE SURE I HAVE SEEN THE
> MISERY OF MY PEOPLE IN EGYPT. I HAVE HEARD THEIR CRIES FOR
> DELIVERANCE FROM THEIR HARSH SLAVE DRIVERS. YES, I AM
> AWARE OF THEIR SUFFERING. SO I HAVE COME TO RESCUE THEM
> FROM THE EGYPTIANS AND LEAD THEM OUT OF EGYPT INTO THEIR
> OWN GOOD AND SPACIOUS LAND. IT IS A LAND FLOWING WITH
> MILK AND HONEY—THE LAND WHERE THE CANAANITES,
> HITTITES, AMORITES, PERIZZITES, HIVITES, AND JEBUSITES LIVE.
> THE CRIES OF THE PEOPLE OF ISRAEL HAVE REACHED ME, AND I
> HAVE SEEN HOW THE EGYPTIANS HAVE OPPRESSED THEM WITH
> HEAVY TASKS. NOW GO, FOR I AM SENDING YOU TO PHARAOH.
> YOU WILL LEAD MY PEOPLE, THE ISRAELITES, OUT OF EGYPT."
>
> EXODUS 3:7-10

I don't know how much of the story you recall, but Moses
was not exactly eager to return to Egypt. He had been running
for his *life* the last time he crossed the border, and a man of
his reputation (remember, he had been raised as the son of
Pharaoh's daughter) did not easily slip back into town, even
in the days prior to CNN.

When you experience a flashpoint, you may not be eager to
undertake the ensuing challenge. What, me? Feed the hungry in
my hometown? Heal the hurts of my dysfunctional family? Stop
drinking? Surely, Lord, you're knocking on the wrong door!

Moses felt the same way.

> "BUT WHO AM I TO APPEAR BEFORE PHARAOH?" MOSES ASKED
> GOD. "HOW CAN YOU EXPECT ME TO LEAD THE ISRAELITES OUT
> OF EGYPT?"

Then God told him, "I will be with you. And this will serve as proof that I have sent you: When you have brought the Israelites out of Egypt, you will return here to worship God at this very mountain."

But Moses protested, "If I go to the people of Israel and tell them, 'The God of your ancestors has sent me to you,' they won't believe me. They will ask, 'Which god are you talking about? What is his name?' Then what should I tell them?"

God replied, "I Am the One who always is. Just tell them, 'I Am has sent me to you.'" God also said, "Tell them, 'The Lord, the God of your ancestors—the God of Abraham, the God of Isaac, and the God of Jacob—has sent me to you.' This will be my name forever; it has always been my name, and it will be used throughout all generations.

"Now go and call together all the leaders of Israel. Tell them, 'The Lord, the God of your ancestors—the God of Abraham, Isaac, and Jacob—appeared to me in a burning bush. He said, 'You can be sure that I am watching over you and have seen what is happening to you in Egypt. I promise to rescue you from the oppression of the Egyptians. I will lead you to the land now occupied by the Canaanites, Hittites, Amorites, Perizzites, Hivites, and Jebusites—a land flowing with milk and honey.'"

"The leaders of the people of Israel will accept your message. Then all of you must go straight to the king of

EGYPT AND TELL HIM, 'THE LORD, THE GOD OF THE HEBREWS, HAS MET WITH US. LET US GO ON A THREE-DAY JOURNEY INTO THE WILDERNESS TO OFFER SACRIFICES TO THE LORD OUR GOD.'

"BUT I KNOW THAT THE KING OF EGYPT WILL NOT LET YOU GO EXCEPT UNDER HEAVY PRESSURE. SO I WILL REACH OUT AND STRIKE AT THE HEART OF EGYPT WITH ALL KINDS OF MIRACLES. THEN AT LAST HE WILL LET YOU GO. AND I WILL SEE TO IT THAT THE EGYPTIANS TREAT YOU WELL. THEY WILL LOAD YOU DOWN WITH GIFTS SO YOU WILL NOT LEAVE EMPTY-HANDED. THE ISRA-ELITE WOMEN WILL ASK FOR SILVER AND GOLD JEWELRY AND FINE CLOTHING FROM THEIR EGYPTIAN NEIGHBORS AND THEIR NEIGH-BORS' GUESTS. WITH THIS CLOTHING, YOU WILL DRESS YOUR SONS AND DAUGHTERS. IN THIS WAY, YOU WILL PLUNDER THE EGYPTIANS!" EXODUS 3:11-22

Man, oh, man, did God ever let Moses have it this time! Not only did he tell him to visit people who wouldn't even recall God's name or power, but he also promised hardship and suffering. Not only that, but the land he promised to Moses' people was already occupied by tribes of warriors with fierce-sounding names, and it's probably significant that Moses hadn't run to *them* for comfort during his exile from Egypt.

Sure, God promised silver and gold and other plunder, but he also promised "heavy pressure" and a lot of "striking at the heart" with "all kinds of miracles."

Moses was still trembling from the effect of the burning bush! How were his nerves supposed to handle miracles impressive enough to sway the heart of a stubborn and powerful king? Moses was no simple shepherd—he had been reared in the palaces of Egypt, he had been educated, he *knew* the royal Egyptian mind-set. He read between the lines of God's message, and the promise of plunder wasn't enough to compel him to embrace what he read.

In your flashpoint moment you may see the future as it could be, but fear may hold you back. And the work is likely to be hard—and possibly long and sweaty and backbreaking. Does God really want you to work that hard?

Yes. And his promise is that the reward will be worth the effort.

> BUT MOSES PROTESTED AGAIN, "LOOK, THEY WON'T BELIEVE ME! THEY WON'T DO WHAT I TELL THEM. THEY'LL JUST SAY, 'THE LORD NEVER APPEARED TO YOU.'"
>
> THEN THE LORD ASKED HIM, "WHAT DO YOU HAVE THERE IN YOUR HAND?"
>
> "A SHEPHERD'S STAFF," MOSES REPLIED.
>
> "THROW IT DOWN ON THE GROUND," THE LORD TOLD HIM. SO MOSES THREW IT DOWN, AND IT BECAME A SNAKE! MOSES WAS TERRIFIED, SO HE TURNED AND RAN AWAY.
>
> THEN THE LORD TOLD HIM, "TAKE HOLD OF ITS TAIL." SO MOSES REACHED OUT AND GRABBED IT, AND IT BECAME A SHEPHERD'S STAFF AGAIN.
>
> "PERFORM THIS SIGN, AND THEY WILL BELIEVE YOU," THE LORD TOLD HIM. "THEN THEY WILL REALIZE THAT THE LORD, THE GOD OF THEIR ANCESTORS—THE GOD OF ABRAHAM, THE GOD OF ISAAC, AND THE GOD OF JACOB—REALLY HAS APPEARED TO YOU."
>
> THEN THE LORD SAID TO MOSES, "PUT YOUR HAND INSIDE YOUR ROBE." MOSES DID SO, AND WHEN HE TOOK IT OUT AGAIN,

HIS HAND WAS WHITE AS SNOW WITH LEPROSY. "NOW PUT YOUR HAND BACK INTO YOUR ROBE AGAIN," THE LORD SAID. MOSES DID, AND WHEN HE TOOK IT OUT THIS TIME, IT WAS AS HEALTHY AS THE REST OF HIS BODY.

"IF THEY DO NOT BELIEVE THE FIRST MIRACULOUS SIGN, THEY WILL BELIEVE THE SECOND," THE LORD SAID. "AND IF THEY DO NOT BELIEVE YOU EVEN AFTER THESE TWO SIGNS, THEN TAKE SOME WATER FROM THE NILE RIVER AND POUR IT OUT ON THE DRY GROUND. WHEN YOU DO, IT WILL TURN INTO BLOOD."

EXODUS 4:1-9

After your flashpoint moment, you may find yourself wondering whether God really intends for you to venture into the big wide world to do what he's called you to do. "You want me to work among atheists and agnostics? Surely you're mistaken, Lord. Can't you send me to a quiet little church where I can fold bulletins or something?"

Some of us are called to church ministry—and there's a lot more to it than folding bulletins, to be sure. Others are called to the workaday world or to serve their families at home. But regardless of where we are, we will be among people who either need to be told or reminded that God is alive and all-powerful. And whatever God calls us to do, he will equip us for service—even if it requires him to work miracles of provision. Even then we might be tempted to shrink back and make excuses.

BUT MOSES PLEADED WITH THE LORD, "O LORD, I'M JUST NOT A GOOD SPEAKER. I NEVER HAVE BEEN, AND I'M NOT NOW, EVEN AFTER YOU HAVE SPOKEN TO ME. I'M CLUMSY WITH WORDS."

"WHO MAKES MOUTHS?" THE LORD ASKED HIM. "WHO MAKES PEOPLE SO THEY CAN SPEAK OR NOT SPEAK, HEAR OR NOT HEAR, SEE OR NOT SEE? IS IT NOT I, THE LORD? NOW GO, AND DO AS I HAVE TOLD YOU. I WILL HELP YOU SPEAK WELL, AND I WILL TELL YOU WHAT TO SAY."

BUT MOSES AGAIN PLEADED, "LORD, PLEASE! SEND SOMEONE ELSE."

THEN THE LORD BECAME ANGRY WITH MOSES. "ALL RIGHT," HE SAID. "WHAT ABOUT YOUR BROTHER, AARON THE LEVITE? HE IS A GOOD SPEAKER. AND LOOK! HE IS ON HIS WAY TO MEET YOU NOW. AND WHEN HE SEES YOU, HE WILL BE VERY GLAD. YOU WILL TALK TO HIM, GIVING HIM THE WORDS TO SAY. I WILL HELP BOTH OF YOU TO SPEAK CLEARLY, AND I WILL TELL YOU WHAT TO DO. AARON WILL BE YOUR SPOKESMAN TO THE PEOPLE, AND YOU WILL BE AS GOD TO HIM, TELLING HIM WHAT TO SAY. AND BE SURE TO TAKE YOUR SHEPHERD'S STAFF ALONG SO YOU CAN PERFORM THE MIRACULOUS SIGNS I HAVE SHOWN YOU."

EXODUS 4:10-17

Can you imagine arguing with God the way Moses did? In light of the miraculous burning bush, his resistance is hard to imagine. Yet we all defy God every day, arguing with the Almighty about changes we need to make or opportunities we ought to take. We just don't resist him as honestly as Moses did. Instead, we ignore, deny, rationalize, and excuse ourselves from the things God calls us to do. We declare ourselves not worthy or ill-equipped. We buy into the false belief that God can use us only on the basis of our qualifications, rather than in spite of our weaknesses.

About twenty weeks a year, I fly out to speak at fund-raisers in support of a pro-life cause. At these events I share the true story of how I paid for the abortion of my baby when I was in college. I tell the audience about my pain, my shame, and the sense of loss I still feel. I also tell them about my adopted daughter, born of parents who responded with a courage I did not possess when faced with a nearly identical situation.

When these opportunities first arose to speak for pro-life causes, I could have argued with God over the absurdity of my involvement. Now, however, I am glad I didn't refuse the chance to help. Pro-life work has become one of the most important and fulfilling aspects of my life. Still, when I realize that God can use even my worst offense as a means to give life to others, I am humbled and amazed. I'm reminded of Paul, once an ardent hater of Christians, who later wrote:

> YOU KNOW WHAT I WAS LIKE . . . HOW I VIOLENTLY
> PERSECUTED THE CHRISTIANS. I DID MY BEST TO GET RID OF
> THEM. . . . BUT THEN SOMETHING HAPPENED! FOR IT PLEASED
> GOD IN HIS KINDNESS TO CHOOSE ME AND CALL ME, EVEN
> BEFORE I WAS BORN! WHAT UNDESERVED MERCY!
>
> GALATIANS 1:13, 15

When you come to your flashpoint experience, you may feel just like Moses. You may want to cast doubt on yourself, your audience, or even on God. But he will support you and equip you. In time, he may even send you an Aaron to help carry the burden.

PREPARING FOR THE JOURNEY

> THEN MOSES WENT BACK HOME AND TALKED IT OVER WITH
> JETHRO, HIS FATHER-IN-LAW. "WITH YOUR PERMISSION," MOSES
> SAID, "I WOULD LIKE TO GO BACK TO EGYPT TO VISIT MY FAMILY.
> I DON'T EVEN KNOW WHETHER THEY ARE STILL ALIVE."
>
> "GO WITH MY BLESSING," JETHRO REPLIED.
>
> BEFORE MOSES LEFT MIDIAN, THE LORD SAID TO HIM, "DO
> NOT BE AFRAID TO RETURN TO EGYPT, FOR ALL THOSE WHO
> WANTED TO KILL YOU ARE DEAD." EXODUS 4:18-19

A wealth of untold information lies buried in this account of
Moses' conversation with his father-in-law. He didn't say a
word about his supernatural encounter in the desert, but
instead fabricated a story about yearning for a family reunion.
Further, he claimed not to know whether any members of his
family were still alive, even though God had just told him that
Aaron was being prepared to meet him.

After Jethro gave his blessing, Moses prepared his family
for the journey. As they were packing, however, a niggling
fear rose in his soul—was he being foolish? Would his obedience result in death? Then God spoke to him again: "Do not
be afraid. Your life is no longer in danger."

After your flashpoint moment, you may find it difficult to
explain your newfound passion to friends and family. If
they've never experienced something similar, they may scoff
or even discourage you. Although I would never encourage
you to lie, it might be the better part of wisdom to exercise
discretion. Ask the Lord for his discernment. Too often in our

early steps on a new path or direction, we say too much too soon. We sound preachy and insincere as we air out our untested ideas. We need to gain some wisdom and experience before we cast ourselves as experts. Let the new truths in your life age a bit. Like a fine wine, the result will be richer and more satisfying.

If you have already had a flashpoint moment, like Moses you may be packed and ready to enter the challenge of a new life. But before you move forward, take note of an essential reality: After Moses had his flashpoint, when God laid out the road before him, the path did not lead downhill! In fact, after Moses left the wilderness of Midian, nearly every step was an uphill battle, filled with challenges and difficulties. Before his mission was accomplished, Moses would find himself at odds with a powerful king, in conflict with the very people he was sent to deliver, pursued by an army of chariots, and pinned down between the onrushing Egyptian army and the forbidding waters of the Red Sea.

God parted the waters, but only after Moses and the people recognized that the only way anyone was going to survive this journey was with divine aid. We, too, will experience moments when we require the intervention of a living, powerful God. If we stay close to God and persevere, he will part the waters, sweep away the fog, make our paths straight, and even clear the road of obstacles when it's time for us to move ahead.

When God met with Moses at the burning bush, the result was a spiritual flashpoint. In a sense, all flashpoints are spiritual because they burst into flame in the soul. In the moment when an idea begins to resonate in our heart and we think,

Something could be done about this or *Something* must *be done about this,* our soul awakens, stretching to fill its God-designed purpose. All flashpoints have this kind of spiritual impact—they change us from the inside out. Of course, the most empowered flashpoints are those ignited and fueled by the Spirit of God. As mighty as our own deeds might be, "nothing is impossible with God" (Luke 1:37).

FINANCIAL FLASHPOINTS

A FRIEND OF MINE told me about a pastor whose financial flashpoint came disguised as a multimillion dollar judicial judgment against him. It turned out to be one of the greatest blessings God had ever bestowed on his life! To make a long story short, an abortion clinic had sued this peace-loving man and two dozen other people, falsely accusing them of cursing and brutalizing the clinic's patients and employees. In his ruling, the judge declared that the pastor's wages would be garnished until the entire judgment had been paid.

This godly minister calmly told the judge that although he was willing to repay any debt he owed, he was *not* willing to support an abortion clinic with even one penny of his salary. When the owners of the clinic came with a court order to garnish his wages from the church, the pastor resigned and formed a nonprofit ministry, which pays him minimum wage, not garnishable under state law. As a result, he said, God not only blessed his family but also taught him many things about money, eternal rewards, and living by faith.

Jesus put the lesson this way:

> DON'T STORE UP TREASURES HERE ON EARTH, WHERE THEY CAN BE EATEN BY MOTHS AND GET RUSTY, AND WHERE THIEVES BREAK IN AND STEAL. STORE YOUR TREASURES IN HEAVEN, WHERE THEY WILL NEVER BECOME MOTH-EATEN OR RUSTY AND WHERE THEY WILL BE SAFE FROM THIEVES. WHEREVER YOUR TREASURE IS, THERE YOUR HEART AND THOUGHTS WILL ALSO BE. . . .
>
> NO ONE CAN SERVE TWO MASTERS. FOR YOU WILL HATE ONE AND LOVE THE OTHER, OR BE DEVOTED TO ONE AND DESPISE THE OTHER. YOU CANNOT SERVE BOTH GOD AND MONEY.
>
> MATTHEW 6:19-21, 24

Money is not the be-all and end-all of life. It is merely a tool for living, giving, and investing in eternity. Jesus told us to store up our treasures in heaven, but how do we do that? By investing in eternal souls—people. God gives us money to provide for our own needs, yes, but also so that we can meet the needs of others. All the money he sends to us is *his;* our role is to manage his finances faithfully as his stewards.

How would you feel if you had wrapped a precious package, addressed it to a relative, and taken it to the post office, only to discover later that your relative never received your gift because a postal clerk had kept it for himself? You'd be frustrated, maybe even outraged. Now look at your financial resources from God's perspective. The principle is the same.

My friend Luci Swindoll often refers to a lesson she

learned from her father. "Daddy always told me," she says, "that I'd always have money and always enjoy my money if with every dollar I received I spent some, saved some, tithed some, invested some, and gave some away. And he was right."

In our giving we not only share financial resources but also the love and compassion of Christ. The world will know we are Christians by our love, and giving is love made tangible. When considering how much money to give to others, people who have experienced a financial flashpoint will not ask, "How much can I keep this month?" but "How much more can I *give?*"

SPIRITUAL ECONOMICS

How we manage our finances is so interwoven with the quality of our spiritual life that the Bible contains more than two thousand references to money, compared to only about five hundred references to prayer. A proper view of money is built on a foundation of spiritual truth. Writer Randy Alcorn makes a similar connection between our finances and our spirituality in his book *Money, Possessions, and Eternity:*

> The enigma deepens when we look at how closely Jesus linked money to salvation itself. When Zaccheus said he would give half his money to the poor and pay back four times over those he had cheated, Jesus did not merely say, "Good idea." He said, "Today salvation has come to this house" (Luke 19:9). This is amazing. Jesus judged the reality of this man's salvation based on his willingness, no, his cheerful *eagerness*

to part with his money for the glory of God and the good of others.[1]

Solomon, the wisest and richest man who ever lived, had strong opinions about finances:

> THOSE WHO LOVE MONEY WILL NEVER HAVE ENOUGH. HOW ABSURD TO THINK THAT WEALTH BRINGS TRUE HAPPINESS! THE MORE YOU HAVE, THE MORE PEOPLE COME TO HELP YOU SPEND IT. SO WHAT IS THE ADVANTAGE OF WEALTH—EXCEPT PERHAPS TO WATCH IT RUN THROUGH YOUR FINGERS!
>
> PEOPLE WHO WORK HARD SLEEP WELL, WHETHER THEY EAT LITTLE OR MUCH. BUT THE RICH ARE ALWAYS WORRYING AND SELDOM GET A GOOD NIGHT'S SLEEP.
>
> THERE IS ANOTHER SERIOUS PROBLEM I HAVE SEEN IN THE WORLD. RICHES ARE SOMETIMES HOARDED TO THE HARM OF THE SAVER, OR THEY ARE PUT INTO RISKY INVESTMENTS THAT TURN SOUR, AND EVERYTHING IS LOST. IN THE END, THERE IS NOTHING LEFT TO PASS ON TO ONE'S CHILDREN. PEOPLE WHO LIVE ONLY FOR WEALTH COME TO THE END OF THEIR LIVES AS NAKED AND EMPTY-HANDED AS ON THE DAY THEY WERE BORN.
>
> ECCLESIASTES 5:10-15

C. S. Lewis was right when he said, "He who has God and everything has no more than he who has God alone."[2] Everything on this earth—cars, houses, gold and silver—will pass away. As Robert Frost says in one of his poems, "Nothing gold can stay." The only things that will endure throughout eternity are eternal things: the Word of God and human souls.

SPENDING WISELY HERE AND NOW

A friend of mine told me about a dream in which she was shopping a clearance rack and picked up a lovely cashmere sweater in teal, her favorite color. The price was $100—a pretty good deal, she assured me, for cashmere. She didn't *need* the sweater, but it was a bargain. As she was thinking how well that sweater would match her eyes, a quiet voice spoke to her heart: "One hundred dollars would sponsor a World Vision child for more than one hundred days." Without hesitation, she put the sweater back on the rack.

When she awoke, she went downstairs, logged on to the World Vision Web site on her computer, and clicked on "sponsor a child." As the first child's picture appeared, she was beginning to wonder if what she had experienced was an ordinary dream or a nudging from the Lord. Then her gaze fell upon the little boy's birthday—it was the same as hers! Confident now that she was acting on an impulse born of the Spirit, she sponsored not one child but two.

Financial flashpoints bring us face-to-face with the realization that God's eternal kingdom is more important than our financial security—that it truly is "more blessed to give than to receive." For many of us it might take a financial flashpoint to teach us how to live within our means. Perhaps then we'll discover better ways to allocate our money instead of knocking ourselves out to accumulate more.

MY GUCCI FLASHPOINT MOMENT

God has taught me a lot about finances over the years, and some of those lessons have been more expensive than others.

While in college, I worked in a clothing store to help meet expenses. The store sold conservative business clothing, and the experience shaped my tastes; I have been a conservative dresser ever since. I have also been a fairly frugal shopper. Most of my khakis come from Costco and cost less than twenty dollars. Buying something at even a Banana Republic would be a splurge for me. Once, I was thrilled to find a cashmere-blend overcoat at Costco for less than one hundred dollars. It was perfect for me, and I still have it.

Then, one day a colleague of mine purchased an Armani suit to celebrate some major life event. When I saw my associate in that expensive, good-looking outfit, well, I'll admit it— I was jealous.

Jealousy soon led me to wonder if I wasn't "undersuiting" myself. Was I not entitled to an expensive designer suit? Evaluation rolled into determination, and within a day or two I found myself at a Gucci store, trying on suits that cost at least three times as much as anything in my closet. The sleek fabric gleamed in the light! Almost like taffeta.

After some consideration, I bought a green one, congratulating myself on my good taste and anticipating the boatload of frequent flier miles that would soon be credited to my American Airlines Visa. Boy, was I proud of that suit!

The first time I wore it, however, at a dinner, a silver dollar-sized spot of salad dressing landed on my right pant leg. In the blink of an eye, I went from feeling like a king to feeling self-conscious and awkward. I walked around the rest of the night with my pant leg twisted to hide the spot on my good-looking, expensive, salad-stained Gucci suit.

The next day, I took the suit to the cleaners and told them

my story. Well, they got the spot out, but when they pressed the jacket, the part that was supposed to be smooth and shiny came out dimpled and rippled. The dry cleaner told me the jacket was ruined because of the way it was made. Back at the Gucci store, the salesman told me the jacket was ruined because of the way it had been pressed.

Back home, my wife—well, she didn't have to say a word. I hung that suit up in the closet and never wore it again. In all my days of average-priced suits, I had never experienced so much trouble. And every day as I passed my new icon of waste in the closet, I wondered if God was trying to teach me a lesson about earthly treasures.

By the way, treasures aren't always something you buy at a shopping mall. In *USA Today,* Craig Wilson points out that luxury, or treasure, is all in the mind of the beholder: "I'm much more jealous of someone's raspberry bush than their jewelry," he says. "Anyone can have diamonds. Not everyone has a raspberry bush."[3] He goes on to define his idea of luxury:

> Pure luxury is time to read the whole paper in the morning, time to take long walks with the dog, time to have long lunches with friends on rainy afternoons when there's no place to go, no schedule to keep. Better than a rushed breakfast at Tiffany's any day. . . . A clothesline, rain on the roof, a steady wind in your sails, a good old-fashioned snowstorm, especially if you live where you don't get one every week. Add a roaring fire, a jigsaw puzzle and the inability to go anywhere for a couple of days, and it doesn't get much better than that.[4]

THE TREASURE PRINCIPLE

Proverbs 23:5 warns that "riches can disappear as though they had the wings of a bird!" So the next time you buy a suit or a sweater or a car, imagine it sprouting wings and taking flight—because it will, you know. The scientific law of entropy guarantees that everything deteriorates. The item you buy today will probably be worth much less tomorrow. If not tomorrow, then in a thousand years. Don't get me wrong. For most people, buying a nice sweater or a nice suit is perfectly okay, *if it meets a need*. But if we don't need something, if it's just one more possession to toss on the pile, there are better ways to spend our money. Randy Alcorn put matters into perspective for me when he explained "the treasure principle":

> Financial planners tell us, "When it comes to your money, don't just think three months ahead, or three years. Think thirty years ahead." Christ, the ultimate investment counselor, takes it further. He says, "Don't just ask how your investment will be paying off in thirty years. Ask how it will be paying off in thirty *million* years."
>
> Suppose I offer you $1000 to spend today however you want. Not a bad deal. But suppose I give you a choice—you can either have that $1000 today, *or* you can have ten million dollars five years from now. Only a fool would take the $1000 today. Yet that's what we do whenever we grab onto what will only last for a moment, forgoing something far more valuable we could enjoy later for much longer.

> The money God entrusts to us here on earth is
> eternal investment capital. Every day is an opportu-
> nity to buy up more shares in his kingdom.[5]

Take a moment to do a little exercise with me. Close your eyes
and consider this question: What sort of work would you do if
all that mattered was what you did, not how much you earned?

What did you envision? Would you still be in your present
job, your present circumstances? Or would you have moved
on to something more fulfilling?

John Gray, communication expert and author of *Men Are
from Mars, Women Are from Venus,* says that we should work as
if money doesn't matter. "When we work mainly for money
instead of for the joy work brings and the contribution we can
make, we lose touch with our deeper needs. Periodically ask
yourself, 'How would I spend my time if I did not need
money?' By keeping this in mind, you will gradually move
in the direction of your dreams."[6]

FLASHPOINT: MAKING THE MOST OF THE TIME YOU HAVE LEFT

Ever since he was seventeen, Quart Graves, a corporate executive in Sugar Land, Texas, has known he is dying. While in
high school, Graves learned that he had pheochromocytoma,
a rare form of adrenal cancer. In 1997, a doctor delivered
devastating news: The cancer had metastasized to Graves's
liver and would keep growing. He had a one in three chance
of living another five years. In 1998 he had several tumors
removed from his liver, but others remain. He had a kidney
removed in 1999. Over the past twenty-two years, Graves has

endured eight life-threatening surgeries. At the age of forty, he does not know how much longer he has to live, but he does know that his disease continues to spread.

After his latest major surgery, Graves was approached by a friend, who asked him to consider changing jobs to become a vice president at Digital Consulting. Taking the job would require a pay cut and the loss of substantial perks, not to mention starting over with a new company in what would probably be the sunset of Graves's life.

As he recuperated from surgery, Graves considered his friend's offer and came to a flashpoint. He decided that God wanted him to use his talents to help other people make money. "Staying at [my old job] would have been an easy way to live out my final days," he said. "Leaving was a risk, and I felt that I would have to trust God more than ever. It was like a test."

Now happily at work in a position where he feels God has placed him, Graves is ready for anything. "I'm called to be a servant of God, a light among the darkness, a salt among the earth. . . . I go where God goes." Graves told a reporter for the *New York Times* that God wants him in the corporate world for now, but one day he might become a minister, manage the finances of a large church, or run an evangelistic organization. "Probably the greatest passion in my life is evangelism," he said.[7]

With a renewed purpose and passion in his life, Quart Graves is ready for anything the future holds. Furthermore, he has learned what God wants us all to understand: Just because he puts money in our hands doesn't mean he intends for it to stay there!

TRUE CONTENTMENT IS GREAT WEALTH

Don't listen to people who tell you that God wants all his children to be rich—that's just not true. In fact, the apostle Paul had much to say on the subject:

> THESE PEOPLE ALWAYS CAUSE TROUBLE. THEIR MINDS ARE CORRUPT, AND THEY DON'T TELL THE TRUTH. TO THEM RELIGION IS JUST A WAY TO GET RICH.
>
> YET TRUE RELIGION WITH CONTENTMENT IS GREAT WEALTH. AFTER ALL, WE DIDN'T BRING ANYTHING WITH US WHEN WE CAME INTO THE WORLD, AND WE CERTAINLY CANNOT CARRY ANYTHING WITH US WHEN WE DIE. SO IF WE HAVE ENOUGH FOOD AND CLOTHING, LET US BE CONTENT. BUT PEOPLE WHO LONG TO BE RICH FALL INTO TEMPTATION AND ARE TRAPPED BY MANY FOOLISH AND HARMFUL DESIRES THAT PLUNGE THEM INTO RUIN AND DESTRUCTION. FOR THE LOVE OF MONEY IS AT THE ROOT OF ALL KINDS OF EVIL. AND SOME PEOPLE, CRAVING MONEY, HAVE WANDERED FROM THE FAITH AND PIERCED THEMSELVES WITH MANY SORROWS. I TIMOTHY 6:5-10

The book of James sums it up this way: "Pure and lasting religion in the sight of God our Father means that we must care for orphans and widows in their troubles, and refuse to let the world corrupt us" (1:27).

I discovered how important this verse is when a man I knew died, leaving behind many sad friends and a wonderful family. His legacy was one of laughter and love for the Lord.

Although he was not affluent, he always seemed to have money and know where to get it. His reputation was spotless; everyone regarded him as a man of integrity. At his funeral, the church was packed with many people who had known and loved him.

Not long after the funeral, another side of my friend's character was revealed, a dark side unknown even to his wife. To her horror, creditors began to call, demanding vast sums of money he allegedly owed them. His wife had not known of any debts other than the mortgage. My friend had never discussed finances with her, and she had entrusted all their financial dealings to him.

So now this widow struggles to pay off debts she never knew she owed. My friend's memory has been forever tarnished, his legacy of love and laughter replaced by the blight of deceptive materialism.

Don't buy into the world's acquisitiveness. Don't allow "affluenza" to overtake your family. Giving freely of your resources is the cure for both conditions. If you prove yourself an efficient "postal clerk," willing to deliver God's provision to those who need it, he will entrust you with more to give.

PUTTING OUR WEALTH IN PERSPECTIVE

We've all heard the saying, "You can't take it with you," but I love the fictional story about the rich man on his deathbed who wanted to bargain with God. "I've worked so hard to amass my fortune," he pleaded in prayer, "and I want to take it with me to heaven."

"We don't do that," God said.

"But please," the man begged. "I'm nothing without my money! But if you won't do it for me, do it for my children. They're spoiled rotten, and the money will only make matters worse. Please, Lord, let me bring it to heaven so they'll be spared from a life of indulgence and corruption."

Upon hearing this revised plea, the Lord had mercy and amended his answer. "All right," he said. "You may bring one suitcase with you into heaven. But only one."

The rich man immediately had his wealth converted into gold bricks. He packed his million-dollar treasure into the largest suitcase he could find and stashed it beneath his bed.

A few weeks later, the man drew his last breath. When he opened his eyes in eternity, he found himself standing at the gate to the heavenly Holy City. Panicked, he looked around for his money, then sighed with relief when he saw the suitcase by his side. The Lord had not forgotten his promise.

The angel at the gate, however, had never seen such a thing. "A suitcase?" he said, lifting a snowy brow. "You can't bring anything into heaven with you!"

"I know this isn't the way you usually do things," the rich man answered, "but I have a special arrangement with God."

"I'll have to look inside the suitcase," the angel declared. "This is extremely unconventional."

Perfectly willing, the rich man stepped back while the angel unzipped the bag and took stock of the gleaming gold bricks. The sentry shook his head slightly, then lifted his voice to the Almighty. "Lord," he called out, parting the heavens with his trumpeting voice, "I've got a man here who says he's made a special arrangement with you."

The heavens rumbled back an answer: "What sort of arrangement was that?"

The angel glanced down at the suitcase again, then lifted his eyes. "For some reason, he wants to bring in a load of paving material."

I love that! In heaven, our gold will be worth less than the pavement under our feet! But the things we often overlook—the eternal souls of children, the poor, the underprivileged—those dear souls will be priceless. Learn to value the things of this world the way God values them.

PHYSICAL FLASHPOINTS

4

I COME FROM A FAMILY of fairly large people. When I was growing up, Thanksgiving dinner with my uncles looked like a room full of major appliances gathered around a turkey! Almost everyone present was overweight, and everything on our table seemed to be either fried or served with gravy. I ate what was on my plate and never thought much about it, but looking back I can see that food, love, and relationships were definitely intertwined in my development. The result was that by the time I was twenty-two, I'd managed to pack 210 pounds onto my five-foot-ten-inch frame.

I was ashamed of my body, and it hurt to know that others were laughing at me. I felt I was destined to be heavy all my life, because, after all, I came from a heavy family.

But the summer before my senior year in college, when I had my picture taken for the yearbook, I experienced a flashpoint that changed everything. When I received the proof,

I was stunned to see the overweight, acne-pocked, oily-haired creature in the photograph. I was so ashamed of what I had become, until I realized I didn't have to stay that way. In that flashpoint moment, I recognized that I was responsible for how I looked, and I could make myself look different.

I had heard all the stories about people who lost weight only to regain it later. I was determined not to repeat that pattern because I knew that most people ended up heavier than they were when they started! Instead, I made gradual changes that caused me to see myself in a different light. I began to walk every day. I learned to eat in different patterns. The flashpoint was instantaneous, but the resulting action took some time. With persistence, slowly but surely, the weight began to drop off, my waist narrowed, and the mirror stopped being my enemy.

First I went down to 190 pounds and lived there for a while. A few years later I slimmed down to 175 and stayed at that weight for a few months. In my last stage of weight loss, I moved down to 160, the weight I maintain today. Thinking that others might benefit from what I had learned, I wrote a weight-loss book called *Gentle Eating*. The secret to weight loss, you see, isn't following rules or a plan—any of those will work temporarily. Permanent weight loss occurs when you change your heart and mind before you attempt to change your body.

FLASHPOINT: CHANGING OUR MIND-SET ABOUT OUR BODY

With the amount of energy most Americans expend on diet obsessions, vaccines, checkups, and medical technology, you'd think we'd be the healthiest people in the world. And in one sense you'd be correct. People today rarely die from smallpox or diphtheria, for example. Infant mortality has dropped steadily over the past century, as has the risk of women dying in childbirth. The advent of the refrigerator, which replaced salt as a preservative for many foods, cut the rate of stomach cancer; and the development of the Pap smear test has lowered the rate of cervical cancer by 75 percent. The average life expectancy, which was forty-seven years for a child born at the turn of the twentieth century, now stands at seventy-four years for men and seventy-nine years for women.[1]

But the twentieth century spawned an entire crop of new health hazards. "What we've done," says Dr. William Dietz of the Centers for Disease Control and Prevention, "is replace the diseases of deficiency with diseases of excess." Because as a society we have food in abundance and gadgets to curb our workload, we are suffering from hypertension, heart disease, diabetes, and cancer in unprecedented numbers.[2]

Americans are more obsessed with body image than any other people in the world. Most of us consider ourselves too tall or too short, too thick or too thin. Preschool girls worry about being too heavy, and teenage girls are killing themselves through anorexia and bulimia. I read of one case where social workers actually took a toddler from her parents because she was too heavy! (She has since been returned to her family.)

New Year's Day inspires more diets than any other day— unless, perhaps, you count the day after a woman gives birth. Throughout the month of January, television programs are interrupted with regular commercials for weight-loss programs, while department stores put athletic equipment, running shoes, and sweatpants on sale. Still, studies have shown that more than half of our nation's adults are either moderately or morbidly overweight, as are 25 percent of all children. Doctors are now monitoring young patients for the diseases of old age—such as type II diabetes.[3]

What we need, in part, is to change our mind-set about our body back to a more biblical perspective. The apostle Paul addressed the subject of our body in one of his letters to the Christians living in Corinth:

> DON'T YOU KNOW THAT YOUR BODY IS THE TEMPLE OF THE HOLY
> SPIRIT, WHO LIVES IN YOU AND WAS GIVEN TO YOU BY GOD?
> YOU DO NOT BELONG TO YOURSELF, FOR GOD BOUGHT YOU WITH
> A HIGH PRICE. SO YOU MUST HONOR GOD WITH YOUR BODY.
>
> 1 CORINTHIANS 6:19-20

Let's be clear about one thing: Honoring God with our body does not mean we're to be obsessed with physical fitness, but it does mean we're responsible for maintaining our body, because it is the dwelling place of the Spirit of God. We can start by recognizing that God gives us food to support life, not to fulfill it. We eat to live; we don't live to eat!

SAY FAREWELL TO HARMFUL HABITS

Taking care of the physical temple requires giving up unhealthy habits. Smoking causes cancer just as surely as over-eating causes obesity. Drug abuse leads to a weakened system and destroys the body. Yes, ingrained habits and addictions are hard to break, but they can be broken. Find the help you need, and set your mind to creating a new and healthy life.

Maintaining a healthy temple also involves periodic medical checkups, especially as we grow older. Shirley Moretti nursed her husband through cancer, but it wasn't until a beloved niece died unexpectedly at age forty-one that Shirley became motivated to visit a doctor for a checkup and her first mammogram. That appointment saved her life because the doctor discovered cancer in both breasts, but it was still early enough to treat successfully.

After that alarming flashpoint experience, Shirley decided to use her time and her hard-earned knowledge to help others. As a board member of the Foundation for Advancements in Breast Care, Shirley has dedicated herself to educating other women about the disease. As a foundation volunteer, she spends one day a week at the Breast Care Center as a patient services support person counseling newly diagnosed cancer patients.

"I go in and listen to the patients and sit with them when they are diagnosed," she says. "Even though family members come, everyone hears things differently. I understand a little more. And they know I'm a survivor. It helps to see someone else who has gone through it."

Shirley not only mentors breast cancer patients but also their frightened spouses. And she knows that this kind of flashpoint experience can change one's perspective on life. "I no longer bother with the little stuff," she says. "That's not important. What's important is today. I can't seem to run fast enough to get it all done. I *live* the foundation—it's my calling. I want to help other people understand they, too, can survive this. They, too, can live each day and be as good and whole of a person as they were before."

Not only does Shirley counsel others, but she also opens

her home regularly for craft-making sessions. She and other foundation supporters sell their crafts at an annual holiday boutique to help provide funding for the foundation's free early-detection educational services, self-examination classes, and health information fairs.[4]

Why should you care about your physical body? Because God cares about you and he gave you life. Just as we are stewards of the money he supplies, we are stewards of the body he has given us. We only get one body, and our wisdom in managing it will be reflected in our health and the length of our life.

FINDING YOUR OPTIMUM WEIGHT

Part of managing our health is maintaining a healthy weight. If you walk into any bookstore, you'll find shelves and shelves of diet books, but you might as well save your money. The secret of weight loss is no secret at all: Burn more calories than you take in. In other words, eat less, move more. Very simple.

A study from the federal government concludes that "popular diets work—at least in the short term—not because they have any special secrets, but because they force us to eat fewer calories."[5]

"The main thing in weight loss is calories *in* versus calories *out*," says Judith Stern, professor of nutrition and internal medicine at the University of California at Davis, who reviewed the report by the U.S. Department of Agriculture. "People go on fad diets and think, 'This one will be different,' but it never is and their weight rebounds and they move on to the next fad diet."[6]

If weight loss is one of your goals, resolve to lose the

weight slowly. After all, it took time to put those extra pounds on, so allow time to take them off. Set modest, achievable goals with short time frames so you can track your progress. Whatever you do, don't tie your weight loss to a specific event like a class reunion or a wedding. If you do, you'll either give up when time runs short, or you'll put the weight back on as soon as the event has passed.

Please understand this—I am not advocating that you diet down to an unhealthy weight just so you can look like a supermodel. I'm not saying you have to be thin to be acceptable, attractive, or admirable. I only want you to be *healthy*.

How heavy is healthy? Many doctors and dietitians recommend using the Body Mass Index, or BMI, to determine your optimum weight. To calculate your BMI, weigh yourself on an accurate scale, then apply the following formula (you might want to grab a calculator):

> Your weight in pounds x 703
> Divided by your height in inches
> Divided by your height in inches again
> Equals your BMI

So, for example, if you are five feet five inches tall (65 inches) and weigh 145 pounds, your BMI would be 24.12, which is in the "optimal" range.

$$BMI = (145 \times 703) \div 65 \div 65 = 24.12$$

	Female	Male
Optimal BMI:	19.1–25.8	20.7–26.4
Overweight BMI:	25.8–32.2	26.4–31.1
Obese BMI:	over 32.2	over 31.1[7]

UNDERSTANDING OUR
NATIONAL FOOD FETISH

In his excellent book *Your God Is Too Safe,* Mark Buchanan
quotes C. S. Lewis on the subject of sex as an appetite.
Decrying the rise in popularity of the striptease show during
the 1940s, Lewis wrote: "Now suppose you came to a country
where you could fill a theatre by simply bringing a covered
plate onto the stage and then slowly lifting the cover so as to
let everyone see . . . that it contained a mutton chop or a bit
of bacon, would not you think that in that country something
had gone wrong in the appetite for food?"[8]

Buchanan says that this warped perspective on food is
exactly what has happened in the United States—and he's
right. In a single day, how many television commercials
portray steaming, succulent, mouthwatering burgers or pizza?
How many full-color ads are designed to appeal to your stomach and taste buds? Buchanan calls it a kind of "culinary
pornography," then adds, "Our world's most prevalent
iconography depicts food."[9]

In this country and many others, we no longer eat merely
to live. Instead, we eat because we adore eating. But even
though our appetites have been overinflated, we can learn to
restore food to its proper place.

GROUP POWER

Too many of us feel trapped in an overweight body because
we think we're all alone. We too easily buy into the lie that
"it's all up to me," and the *me* I know just doesn't have what
it takes. Our weight bounces all over the scale like a pogo

stick, jarring our emotions at every turn. We want to believe we are acceptable, but we can't deny that the heaviest part of our body is our heart, weighed down with grief, frustration, and shame, smothering our dreams and our hopes for the future. No wonder there are days when we don't want to get out of bed! Our sense of powerlessness produces the horrible fear that we may never get better.

If you have been in this dark place, you know the pain and suffering, and the feeling of being misunderstood. Normal weight people tell us to pull ourselves together, snap out of it, and stop feeling sorry for ourselves. "Think positively," one person will say, while another exclaims, "Just diet!"

If losing weight were that simple, we would have reached our goals long ago. We have obsessed over every quick-fix diet and superficial solution. We know that snapping, pulling, and dieting are powerless to help us look and feel the way that God intended for us to look and feel.

When I carried fifty extra pounds, I lugged around an equal weight of regret, shame, and inferiority. I carried those feelings wherever I went and plopped them down for everyone to see. I was judged for my excess weight and always made to feel like a second-class loser who was too undisciplined to control himself. I dreaded summer because I knew that people would see me in a swimsuit and look at me in disgust. Even if they were kind enough to pretend they didn't notice, I knew they did. And I could do nothing but laugh and try to hide my pain. If liposuction had been a viable option back then, I would have wanted to have my body vacuumed from cheeks to toes. I'm glad now that liposuction wasn't an option, because it wasn't my body that needed repair, it was my broken, disconnected heart.

Like many men, I found it hard to connect with others, and I resisted close relationships at all costs. But someone finally convinced me that I should try attending a group where others shared my feelings. I'm sure that no one dreaded going to that meeting more than I did. When I arrived, I discovered an interesting mix of people. Some were much heavier than I was, and others looked like they had no eating problems at all. True to human nature, I compared myself to the heavy ones and puffed with pride, and I looked on the thin ones with envy. But as they spoke and shared their hearts, I learned that real people lived inside those bodies, and they had all been walking through the same darkness I had.

That night, I was comforted to know I was not alone in my suffering. The bond of shared pain gave me hope that we might be able to help each other. I felt that the least I could do was agree to go back again.

The next week, I returned with anticipation rather than dread. I couldn't wait to discover the mysteries of the other people's lives, even as I unwrapped my own. Oh, the freedom that came as I revealed my secrets, confessed my fears, and expressed my regrets! The acceptance and safety I felt in that group allowed God to gently heal my hurts and sweeten the bitter memories I had been trying to numb with food. Slowly, over time, I felt the power of God coming through those people who cared enough to listen to my rants and guard the secrets of my heart.

With the support and encouragement of that group, I was able to stop seeking comfort in food and start allowing God to comfort me and show me the way to a lighter heart. I know for certain that God wants to do the same for you—no matter what behavior patterns you want to change.

Today there are support groups for every conceivable need—for those who have addictions to food, alcohol, or sex, to those who care for aging parents or children with special needs. Your church may offer several support groups. If not, find a church that does. If you are housebound, there are on-line groups that can provide friendship and encouragement via computer.

Joining a support group might be the most courageous thing you could do right now, and I want to encourage you to take this important step. And don't just attend the meetings—make an effort to connect with the people. They've earned the right to hear your story by sharing theirs. Once you've joined a group, don't quit. Commit yourself to persevere until you have given the group several weeks or months to help you change your destructive patterns.

If you have tried everything else and failed to overcome your challenge, I urge you to try a support group. If you have dropped out of a support group, go back with a different perspective: Trust the other people. Need them. Connect with them. Confess to them. Care about each of them as much as you want them to care about you. If you will do these things, I believe you will find the power of God working through the unity of that group.

When we join a Christian group, a body of believers, we take our place in the body of Christ and fulfill a vital part of our God-given purpose. "So it is with Christ's body," Paul writes. "We are all parts of his one body, and each of us has different work to do. And since we are all one body in Christ,

we belong to each other, and each of us needs all the others"
(Romans 12:5).

Hebrews 10:24 encourages Christians to "think of ways to
encourage one another to outbursts of love and good deeds."
I love that! As we encourage each other in unity and love,
God begins to transform us from the inside out. Inner transformation—isn't that really what we want?

STRENGTHENING THE BODY

Several years ago, I had another physical flashpoint—one that
has brought me considerable enjoyment. Now that I was "thin
within," I decided to work on my fitness as well. The daily
walk I had incorporated into my lifestyle almost thirty years
before became a jog, then a run. As I pushed myself, my
endurance increased to the point where I could successfully
complete the Big Sur Marathon. Running in that marathon
was a great thrill, and training for it with friends was even
better. But when I arrived back home I realized that all my
running had done little to strengthen my overall body. So I
began to lift weights occasionally. Starting in 1999, I made it
a habit to visit the gym three days a week whenever possible.
The results of my weight-lifting program have been phenomenal. You'd never mistake me for Arnold Schwarzenegger, but
the few pounds of muscle I added made a major difference in
my metabolism. I noticed that I could eat more and maintain
my weight or eat the same amount as before and lose weight.
Obviously, I was burning more calories throughout the day.
Not only did my body look better than it ever had before, but
today I feel better than at any other time in my life.

Most people who meet me today would not believe that

I ever struggled with a weight problem. But I did, and that's why I know that you, too, can be successful at bringing your weight under control. I want to encourage you to broaden your vision of who you can be and what you can do. Your physical flashpoint might come as the result of a quick glance in the mirror, the completion of an entire bag of cookies, or having to use a seatbelt extension on an airplane. If you are like me, when your flashpoint comes, you will be just as motivated to improve as you were to eat. Your passion will shift from consumption to conversion. Before long you'll have gained control of *what* you eat, *why* you eat, and *how* you treat your physical body.

Do you believe me? I hope you do, because your mind may be the only thing that stands in the way of your new body and your new hope. If you want to begin an exercise program, here are a few ideas to help you get off to a good start.

1. First, see your doctor before beginning any exercise program. He or she will be able to certify that you're healthy and maybe even give you tips about what exercise will be best for you as you begin.
2. Be honest about what you enjoy doing. If you hate to run, forget about jogging—take up dancing instead. The goal is movement, and there are a hundred different ways to move.
3. Be open to new ideas. For a period of two or three weeks, try a variety of different exercises: walking, aerobic exercising with a video, dancing, bicycling—whatever you can think of. Discover what you really enjoy.

4. Decide whether you'd do best in solo or corporate exercise. Some people love the motivation and camaraderie of a group; others prefer to sweat alone.

5. Make an exercise appointment, and mark it on your calendar. Once you become used to the schedule, you'll feel something's missing if you skip your exercise "date."

6. Set aside some money—you'll need it, if only for a good pair of exercise shoes—but don't blow a small fortune on exercise equipment for your home until you've tried it somewhere else and you're sure you'll use it. Hint: Check the classified ads and yard sales for bargains from folks who bought equipment before they made regular exercise a habit!

7. Use rhythmic music. Movement is easier when you have a beat urging you forward. If you're working on a treadmill or exercise bike, find something to take your mind off the repetitive motion. One of my friends reads on the exercise bike and watches movies while on the treadmill. If the movie's good, she says, she scarcely notices how hard she's working!

8. Keep setting new goals as you progress. Once you can walk a mile in twenty minutes, press toward the goal of walking that same mile in fifteen. Once you can do thirty sit-ups, set a new goal of forty.

9. Work slowly at first, especially if you're coming out of a sedentary lifestyle. Don't expect to run a marathon after two weeks of training. It took me six months to prepare for the Big Sur Marathon, and I started my preparation in fairly good shape because I had already been exercising for a while. Just take it slow and easy, and don't give up.

10. Finally, work exercise into your life. Don't drive around for twenty minutes hoping for a perfectly convenient parking spot; park at the back of the lot and walk to the store! Don't take the elevator when you can take the stairs, and don't just tap your foot to the music when you can clap, too!

CAREER FLASHPOINTS

5

A FRIEND OF MINE used to teach twelfth-grade English in a Christian school. One day, in a unit on English as a career, she asked her students what considerations might motivate their career selection. Money was the top answer, followed by talent, ability, and a general liking for the type of work. "Are you saying," she asked her class, "that none of you have considered your future occupation in the light of what God would have you do?"

Sadly, many people think that unless they've received "a calling" to become a minister or a missionary, God can pretty much stay out of the career picture. But God calls dentists, too, and salesclerks, insurance salesmen, and corporate executives. If we don't consult him about our career choices, we might make a serious mistake.

Whatever our chosen occupation might be, we should see it as a calling from God. And then, as Solomon advised,

65

"Whatever you do, do well. For when you go to the grave, there will be no work or planning or knowledge or wisdom" (Ecclesiastes 9:10).

As one man said, "Religious activity, Bible study, our personal devotions must be a preparation, not a substitution, for dealing with pivotal choices facing all of us: What am I giving my life to? Do my goals, ambitions, and values reflect the beliefs I espouse? How much of what I consider important does God consider valuable in light of eternity?"[1]

Dorothy Cantor, psychologist and author of *What Do You Want to Do When You Grow Up?* says that people often regret their career choices midstream. One of her clients, a stockbroker, told her: "What I have done as work has absolutely no redeeming social value." Another client, a nursing supervisor, told Cantor, "I think it will be a terrible thing if I hit my old age without ever having done something bold, difficult, or dangerous. I need to be a little rash."[2]

Sometimes "being rash" means not working outside the home at all. If you're a parent, you may feel called to buck the current trend and stay home to raise your children. Other parents have designed careers they can fulfill from home, enabling them to be available to their children whenever they're needed.

Whether you receive a paycheck or emotional reward for your job, can you honestly say that God has directed you to your present work? Did you seek his guidance before or since taking your present job or position? If not, perhaps it's time you did! You may find that he directed your path without your knowledge, or you might discover that he has some other work in mind for you.

How do we find the work that God wants us to do? First, we should take stock of our gifts and abilities. Most people enjoy doing things that exercise their gifts. Second, we can ask friends, coworkers, and family members if they have any particular feeling about what kind of work we might enjoy. Finally, we can take a test such as the Myers-Briggs Type Indicator. Don't worry, it isn't the kind of test you can pass or fail, but you can gain insights into the way you were created, and you'll understand why certain types of work will suit you better than others. You may even discover some latent strengths you've never before exercised! (You can find information on the Myers-Briggs Type Indicator in many books, including *What Type Am I?* by Renee Baron.)

American history is filled with examples of men and women who had midcareer flashpoints and decided to see the resulting decision through. Although most of their names will be unfamiliar to you, your life has no doubt been affected by what they accomplished. For example:

- Malcom McLean, a trucker, came up with the idea of putting cargo in large, uniform metal containers for transport. After battling tradition, rail companies, and unions, McLean increased the efficiency of global shipping.

- Victor Gruen, an immigrant from Austria, was hired to build an American shopping center in the mid-1950s. In a flashpoint moment, he envisioned two stores sharing a common roof—and created the first shopping mall.

- Alexander Poniatoff, a former pilot in the Russian military, came to America and in 1944 founded a company he called Ampex. The new company had nothing to do with aircraft. Under his leadership and vision, a pair of creative geniuses created the first videotape recorder.

- Marcian "Ted" Hoff, an engineer with Intel Corporation, managed to fit the logic unit of a mainframe computer onto a chip the size of a fingernail. He and others at Intel weren't certain what could be done with the tiny chip, so they invited the world to try it on for size. Intel did not obtain patent rights, and Hoff never became wealthy from his invention, but today you'll find a microprocessor in everything from your desktop computer to your toaster.[3]

BALANCING LIFE AND WORK

No matter what your job might be, never confuse quantity with quality. Don't think you must become a workaholic to make your efforts count. Studies have shown that people can work long hours for only so long before they suffer a loss of productivity. "Balancing work and personal time," says Elaine St. James, a leading expert on simplicity, "makes life more enjoyable and could improve job performance."[4]

Sometimes we have to schedule relaxation to be able to enjoy it. Set aside a "sabbath," a day on which you will do no regular work, and if staying late is a problem, resolve to leave work "on time" at least two nights a week.

Look at your weekly calendar and evaluate the meetings you have scheduled. Elaine St. James suggests that we would benefit by resigning from any organization whose meetings stir up a feeling of dread. "Over time," she says, "we all accumulate obligations. Some are unavoidable. . . . Others just feel unavoidable. If you don't enjoy participating and don't get anything out of it, spend your time on something else."[5]

Here's the bottom line: If you're attending a function just because other people expect you to be there, or if you're just "filling a chair," it's probably a waste of your time. Free yourself by declining those meetings in the future.

WHEN YOU FIND YOURSELF OUT OF A JOB

One quick note about the flashpoint commonly known as *being fired* or *laid off:* If you lose your job, don't give up. Don't let your release from employment be a release from life!

The other day, I was talking to a man about his experience of being fired from a job. After the initial shock had worn off, he grieved for a while, and then he sat around the house—and did *nothing.* Because he had considerable savings, he did not have to work, so he didn't. Staying home became easier and easier.

That was ten years ago, and now his savings have been depleted. Being fired left him without employment, but his self-imposed sabbatical left him without self-respect. Now he doesn't know what to do with himself, and his decade-long period of relaxation has left him ill-equipped and unprepared for today's job market.

If you lose your job, don't drop out of the race. Hang in

there. Find a job, any respectable job, to keep yourself sharp while you continue to look for work that matches your God-given skills, interests, and aptitudes. If you have a job, don't retire until you are too weak to work, especially if you are a man. The mortality rate for newly retired men is startling. (Ladies, here's a hint: If your husband is retired, don't let him sit around watching television or doing nothing. It's bad for his health, and in time, you'll both go crazy!)

FLASHPOINT: RELOCATE OR RESIGN

Employment imparts strength and self-respect, even if we're not working at our dream job. Work also keeps us depending on God.

I once spoke to a woman named Kaye who moved across the country to accept a senior position at a publishing house. One of her reasons for accepting the job was that the company would allow her to live and work in another town a few hours away. The situation seemed ideal. Her editorial work did not demand daily face-to-face contact, and moving enabled her to live near her aging parents.

After a few years of successful employment, however, the head of the company decided to bring all staff in-house. Kaye was told that she'd either have to move close enough to commute or resign.

"My first flashpoint came when I heard 'relocate or resign,'" Kaye says. "And for twenty-four hours I reeled in hurt, anger, and a sense of betrayal. Being able to live near my parents, to be there for them when they really needed me, was a huge factor in my accepting the job, and to have that taken away—well, it cut deep.

"Ironically, because my husband is self-employed, my job gave us the stable income and the insurance. For years I had said, 'If I ever lose my job, we're in trouble.' Suddenly my worst-case scenario was happening before my eyes, and for a few hours I wasn't sure whether my employer or God had gone crazy.

"For a full day I was numb with grief and shock, then I called some people to ask for advice about going to work as a freelance editor. The encouragement I encountered was amazing. One person even said, 'Hallelujah! I've thought for years you should freelance.' My husband and I set up an appointment with my employer, then drove over to meet with him, talking and praying the whole way, asking God to go before us and bring about reconciliation. For three hours we talked, and after a lot of tough words and honest emotion, the reconciliation came. Not with the job, per se, but with a person both my husband and I had considered a friend as well as an employer. And that meant a great deal.

"We left that meeting in a spirit of peace and restoration, even though my employment situation was still uncertain. The next day, however, my boss called and said that he'd spoken to a trusted advisor who assured him that if I had *believed* we had a covenant arrangement, we *had* a covenant arrangement. So he would gladly honor that arrangement, and I could continue working for the company from my home.

"Then came the next flashpoint—at that moment, it was as if God put his hand on my shoulder and whispered, 'It's time.' Even though I now had the freedom to keep my job *and* my home, I sensed it was time to move on—not an easy thing for a woman like me to say. I like security, you see. I like knowing where my paycheck is coming from.

"But in working as a freelance editor, I've learned so many things. I've learned that my security lies in God, not in a job. I've also learned that knowing God is faithful to provide doesn't keep you from being human and fearful. It's a constant process of choosing to trust.

"I feel as if I'm walking in a pitch-black cave. It's so dark I can't see my hand in front of my face. And if I reach out, I can't touch the person in front of me, but I know he's there because I can hear his voice: 'One step to the left. Good. Now, one step to the right.'

"Sometimes I'm nearly paralyzed by fear, and in those moments I have to focus on God's voice. He is always there, and he has never failed me. But for a person who likes being able to see down the road, this sort of experience is a challenge. It's also a joy, because daily God proves himself faithful."

FLASHPOINT: THE "GOING NOWHERE" BLUES

Ina Garten had worked at the White House for four years in the Office of Management and Budget. Her field of expertise? Nuclear policy. Then one day she had a flashpoint. "I just couldn't do it anymore," she told *Fast Company* magazine. "I hated that I worked on something for four years without seeing anything happen."[6]

Resigning her position, Garten made the decision to apply her energies to a new enterprise. Today, she is the owner of

Barefoot Contessa, a specialty-foods store in East Hampton, New York, and she has authored a cookbook.

FLASHPOINT: SEEING LIFE FROM ANOTHER PERSPECTIVE

Flashpoints can come at any stage in life. When Pattie Moore was seventeen years old, she was a promising student at the Rochester Institute of Technology, living away from home for the first time and trying to balance homesickness with her strong drive and ambition. One day as the city bus she was riding through downtown Rochester stopped for a traffic light at a busy intersection, an old man on the sidewalk caught Moore's attention. "He was disheveled, but clean," she later recalled, "and he carried two loaded shopping bags, one under each arm. I could see the deliberateness of each step and the strain of his load. I just sat there in tears, watching. Seeing him was like ice water in the face for me." It was a flashpoint experience, awakening in Moore an awareness that older people need special attention.

A spirit of altruism, the unselfish regard for the welfare of others, soon became an important motivator in Pattie Moore's life. After graduation in the mid-1970s, she moved to New York City and accepted a job with the prestigious industrial design firm of Raymond Loewy. As she began to develop products, the insight she had gained from her experiences led her to design products with older people in mind. To guide her efforts, she considered her work from the perspective of her beloved grandfather, a man she called "Dutch." With each assignment she would ask herself, *Could my grandfather manage this with his aging eyes and hands?*

Moore's love for her grandfather motivated her to create objects that would be manageable for elderly people, but a chance meeting—and another flashpoint—inspired her to take an enormous risk that greatly deepened her understanding of the plight of our senior citizens. After meeting Barbara Kelly, a makeup artist for the NBC television network, Moore decided to spend several months disguised as an old woman in order to discover for herself how America treated the elderly.

With Kelly's help, Moore determined that she would not only look old but she would *feel* old. While Kelly fit latex pieces to Moore's twenty-six-year-old face, Moore wrapped her legs with Ace bandages, then wore support stockings over them to bind her movements. She put wax in her ears to replicate the loss of hearing that comes with age and drops of baby oil in her eyes to cloud her vision. She wrapped adhesive tape around her fingers to simulate arthritis, and then wore gloves over the tape. Dressed as an elderly woman, she went out into the world to shop, travel, and observe.

During her numerous forays into the world as an "elder," Pattie Moore learned what it is like to be ignored, shoved, mugged, cheated, and ostracized. Often she was treated rudely. Once she was badly beaten. "When I was in character, if I got a smile or a hello from a passerby, I felt like I'd received a hug from God himself," she recalled.

From her experiments in disguise, Moore learned to accept each moment of life as it comes. "I used to follow my mother's philosophy of saving for a rainy day, but I've been cautioned by my elders that living fully for today is more important. You shouldn't be haphazard, but if there's a regret I hear from my elders it's that they didn't do enough living when they were younger. Don't save up for that ultimate dream, they tell younger people, but live each moment as it comes."

Moore's experiment helped to change not only her own thinking about the elderly but the thinking of industrial designers, politicians, and others who learned about her work. Pattie Moore's flashpoint, and her decision to undertake a grand experiment, improved the lives of countless aging Americans.

FLASHPOINT: A SUDDEN AWAKENING

Denise Stinson is a literary agent in Detroit. She is also an African-American. One day it dawned on her that even though Christianity had long been a dynamic force within the African-American tradition and culture, no mainstream publishing house had devoted an imprint to black Christian fiction.

Stinson's flashpoint realization led her to establish a small publishing house for black Christian fiction. In 2000, she entered into a partnership with Warner Books to create an imprint called Walk Worthy Press. As owner and publisher of the imprint, she handles acquisitions, but she maintains a wall of separation between her publishing role and her literary agency by not selling her own clients' work to Walk Worthy.

Stinson's initial acquisition, a first novel by Victoria Christopher Murray titled *Temptation,* had a first printing of 20,000 copies. The second title, *Singsation* by Jacquelin Thomas, also debuted with a print run of 20,000 copies. Stinson hopes to produce six novels each year and eventually expand into

Christian nonfiction as well, all aimed at an African-American audience. Statistics have shown that 75 percent of African-American book buyers also read Christian books.

"Warner was open, interested, and willing to take a chance with me," she says. "Some other publishers have African-American imprints of general books, but a lot of what they are doing is trade paperback, which is low risk. Our books are hardcover."

Jamie Raab, publisher of Warner Books, is delighted by Walk Worthy's prospects. "Denise came to us with this really strong vision, and we knew she knew the market better than anyone else. When you come across someone with a vision like this . . . you want to be a part of it."

Says Martin Arnold, a writer for the *New York Times,* "Until fairly recently there were only two major book companies committed to publishing lines of fiction (not romances) and nonfiction by black writers on black subjects. Now there are five. Hello, it was as if publishing had suddenly awakened to the idea that African-Americans will buy great numbers of books if the stories . . . are relevant to them."[7] "A sudden awakening" is another way to describe a flashpoint.

FLASHPOINT: A NEW MISSION

As a young man American film director Robert Flaherty spent many grueling months journeying to the Far North in a search of iron ore and cod. He found neither, but in the course of his travels he shot more than 70,000 feet of film. To salvage something from the enterprise, Sir William Mackenzie, a Canadian financier, encouraged Flaherty to edit the film and create a documentary.

For weeks he toiled in a garret room, piecing together bits and pieces of footage into a sensible and effective film. Finally, after hours of concentrated labor, he produced an edited motion picture. Lighting a cigarette in celebration, he dropped the match on the floor, where an ash ignited the cellulose nitrate base on a pile of film negatives. The room instantly became a roaring inferno, and every scrap of the highly flammable celluloid was destroyed. Badly burned in the effort to save his work, Flaherty finally had to jump through a window and barely escaped with his life.

Robert Flaherty came to a literal flash point—and made a decision that would change the course of filmmaking. He resolved to return to the Far North and make a film of Eskimo life "that people will never forget." He did, and the result was the classic documentary *Nanook of the North,* a landmark film in the history of the documentary movement.[8]

FLASHPOINT:
TIME TO PURSUE MY PASSION

Renee Zellweger was born in Houston, studied at the University of Texas at Austin, and worked her way through college as a waitress. She discovered her love for acting in a speech class. "I enjoyed having that moment during the day where we went and expressed something," she says. Her first role in a commercial led to tiny roles in six movies, then she drove to Hollywood to try and make it on her own.

After arriving in Los Angeles, Zellweger found that the doors of opportunity did not open easily. She worked as a waitress again and acted in a few little-known films. Things took a turn for the worse when a former boyfriend in Austin killed himself. Then her agent suggested that she audition for the film *Jerry Maguire*. The opportunity "came at a time when I was at a crossroads in my life, and there was not a lot of light," she says. "It was a transition period, a sad period." Nevertheless, Zellweger made the decision to persevere in her passion—and she won the part. She went on to make other movies, win a Golden Globe award, and is now one of Hollywood's most appealing young actresses.[9]

FLASHPOINT: SELF-DISCOVERY

You may be familiar with Phil McGraw, the "tell it like it is" doctor who regularly appears on Oprah Winfrey's talk show. He may appear confident, but Dr. Phil wasn't born knowing who he was. He engaged in a lot of experimentation before he found his niche and the woman who boosted him to success.

McGraw worked in private psychotherapy practice for ten years but found the job did not bring him personal fulfillment. "Somebody comes to you and says, 'I'm depressed,'" he told *USA Today*. "So you work with them for six months. Are they better, or are they worse? Well, you didn't have a very accurate measure. It's not like you had a quart-and-a-half of depression and now it's down to a pint. It was very frustrating for me."

He began to look for other ways to use his degree: He ran a pain clinic, worked in corporate management training, and did airline consulting with stressed-out pilots. Because he's an expert in the brain and central nervous system, he often found himself called on to testify at trials and other court proceedings.

During this period, McGraw took a long, hard look at himself, weighed his strengths and weaknesses, and came to a flashpoint: "I can't sing, I can't dance, I can't draw a straight line, my penmanship is horrible, but what I can do is analyze things really fast—analyze people, situations. And so to go into the legal arena and do trial strategy . . . what better job could you get for a guy like me than that?"

Fired by a passion born from his self-inventory, McGraw established Courtroom Sciences, a company that stages mock trials in order to prepare lawyers for the real event. In 1998, the business was doing well, and then Oprah Winfrey called.

She was being sued by representatives of the cattle industry, who claimed that when she swore off hamburgers in April 1996, their business went down the tubes. She had legal experts galore working on her case, but the *why* of the entire lawsuit eluded and bothered her. She went to Phil McGraw and, with tears in her eyes, asked why she was being sued for fraud, slander, defamation, and negligence, not to mention $100 million in damages.

Dr. Phil took her hand, talked straight to her, and Oprah not only won her case, but she found a friend. Since then, Dr. Phil has become a regular on her show, and his books, including *Life Strategies* and *Relationship Rescue,* have been best-sellers—spurred, of course, by prominent placement on Oprah Winfrey's talk show.

Dr. Phil doesn't mind being known as Oprah's straight-talking analyst. "When I was young," he said, "it was achievement stuff and money. A young lion. You want to conquer the world and make all the money and get all the accolades and get all the stuff. I'd like to think I've expanded my definition of success to not only include, but be dominated by, such things as family and peace."[10]

FLASHPOINT:
"I CAN FIND SOMETHING BETTER"

Sarah Breedlove, later known as Madam C. J. Walker, was
born in Delta, Louisiana, in 1867. Her parents, day laborers
on the same plantation where they had been slaves, were
entrenched in the kind of poverty from which few escape.
Orphaned at the age of seven, Sarah spent the rest of her
childhood living with a cruel brother-in-law and a passive
sister. She married at fourteen in order to escape. At seventeen
she became a mother; at twenty, a widow. In 1888, probably
after a flashpoint, she moved to St. Louis with her little girl,
looking for employment and opportunity.

She found a job as a washerwoman, and for ten years she
moved from boardinghouse to boardinghouse, washing clothes
and linens. And then she came to another flashpoint.

"I was at my washtubs one morning," she said, "and
looked at my arms buried in soapsuds. I said to myself: 'What
are you going to do when you grow old and your back gets
stiff? Who is going to take care of your little girl?' That set me
to thinking, but with all my thinking I couldn't see how I,
a poor washerwoman, was going to better my condition."

Then her hair began to fall out. Seeking a remedy, she
discovered products from the Poro School of Beauty Culture.
Before long, she started selling the products herself and moved
to Denver. Aided by her daughter, she took her Wonderful
Hair Grower across the country, setting up shops, and demon-
strating her techniques for African-American hair care.

What woman doesn't want to look her best? Madam
Walker's formula, when used with a hot metal comb invented
by a Frenchman in 1879, gave hair a resilience and straightness

that allowed black women to wear the popular styles of the day, including the Gibson girl and the flapper's bob cut. By 1907, Walker was making $300 per month (compared to her former income of $300 per year), and was well on her way to becoming one of the richest businesswomen in America.

Madam Walker's passion translated not only into personal success but also into philanthropy. She sought to inspire others, even building a mansion she called "a Negro institution," erected to show her fellow African-Americans "what a lone woman accomplished, and to inspire them to do big things." She became an advocate of economic freedom for African-American women, hiring black women to work in her factory, her executive offices, and her sales force. Her will even stipulated that the company should always be run by a woman.

Madam C. J. Walker changed the way many African-American women viewed themselves—which affected the way the rest of the nation viewed African-American women. All because of a flashpoint that caught fire in the soapsuds of a washtub.[11]

FLASHPOINT:
TURNING PAIN INTO PURPOSE

Texas car dealer Marion Brem is a hard worker, but what makes her success story so remarkable is that it was born out of pain. During a routine gynecological checkup in the early 1980s, Brem's doctor discovered a breast lump and evidence of cervical cancer. After undergoing a hysterectomy, Brem learned that the breast lump was also cancerous; in fact, it was a rare and aggressive form.

To treat the breast cancer, Brem had a mastectomy and underwent a regimen of daily chemotherapy, which left her weak and nauseated. Two years later, she lost her other breast to a second cancerous tumor. Eventually, her marriage failed from the stresses brought on by her illness, leaving her responsible for her two sons, ages fourteen and eight. Further compounding her problems were steep medical bills—as much as $500,000 not covered by insurance. Worse yet, the doctors gave her no more than five years to live.

Even though Brem faced the worst that life could throw at her, she did not give up or lose hope. After completing her chemotherapy, and desperately in need of a job, Brem began visiting auto dealerships in search of work. She had once worked as a telephone receptionist at a dealership and was hoping to capitalize on that experience. By the time she reached the seventeenth dealership on her list, she had stopped asking managers, "Would you consider hiring a woman?" and had begun opening the interview with, "Here's what I can do for you." Finally she met a general manager who sized her up and said, "I've been thinking about hiring a broad lately, and you seem like the nervy type."

One year later, Marion Brem was proclaimed Salesman of the Year and was awarded a man's Rolex watch and tickets to the Super Bowl. Five years later, after finding success in the predominately male field of car sales, she wrote a business plan to open her own dealership and presented it to a Dallas-area accounting firm. A silent partner arranged for the necessary working capital to get her started, and Marion Brem was on her way. Within two years, her dealership grew from seven employees to sixty-five, and she was able to buy out her partner.

Today, with her cancer in remission, Brem works with her two sons in her dealership. The author of a book on women and entrepreneurship, she also owns an ad agency, various real estate properties, and is part owner of a local bank. "Any time you take a tiny peek at death like I did," she says, "you live life with more urgency."[12]

FLASHPOINT:
GETTING IT RIGHT THIS TIME

Forty-year-old Mike Baker always wanted to be his own boss, but in 1997 he was working on the loading dock at a Levi Strauss denim plant for $9.75 an hour. When someone offered him a box of one thousand miscellaneous mass-produced photos for $100, Baker accepted the offer.

He turned to eBay, the largest auction service on the Internet, and discovered that by listing the prints individually, he could earn up to $65 per print. When Levi Strauss closed its denim plant later that year, Baker applied more of his time and energy to his eBay auctions. He soon became an art clearinghouse, buying bulk prints from dealers and reselling them individually on the Internet auction site.

His new pursuit, though profitable, soon devoured his day. Immediately after getting out of bed in the morning, he checked the computer. Right after breakfast he listed his new auctions. Midmorning, he collected the hundreds of checks that poured in, and the afternoon was spent labeling and organizing prints ready to be shipped. He had no time for lunch. Dinner was gulped down in the company of his family, but then he was back at the computer, answering customer e-mails, keeping track of auctions, and straightening out problems with lost shipments.

Fast Company magazine reported that "by early 1999, more than 5,000 customers had posted positive comments about Baker on eBay's site. It earned him a coveted red star on his eBay biography page, . . . [but] in his own household, he wasn't a hero anymore."

"I was up till 1:00 A.M. every night, seven nights a week," Baker told a reporter. "I was getting really stressed out. My kids were telling me to slow down. They kept saying, 'Dad, we never see you. You're at that computer all the time.'"

Finally, Mike Baker came to his flashpoint. Something had to give, and if he wanted to keep his business and maintain peace in the family—and if he wanted to spend time with his children before they grew up and left home—he would have to make some changes. He started by hiring family members to handle the mail, the checks, and the shipping. By the end of the year, he had five people on the payroll, and he was beginning to get to know his wife and children again.

In the process he learned the beauty of a few simple rules. E-mails that weren't answered by 11:30 P.M. could wait until the next day. He could take a break to pick up his daughters from school, and on the way home he promised not to talk about his work. And family would always take priority over business.

I have a feeling that Mike Baker realized what many wise men and women have learned: Passion for business is good, but passion for family is better. A business will help you make a living, but it's in our families that we learn—and teach— how to live.[13]

LIFESTYLE FLASHPOINTS

6

A FEW YEARS AGO, Bill and Deb Kindig discovered that some friends in their neighborhood, Mario and Judy, were putting their house up for sale. When they asked about the situation, they discovered that Mario and Judy were considering a divorce. The news was troubling, but Bill and Deb weren't sure what they should do.

Then Deb had a flashpoint of inspiration and dared to make a difference. Concerned about her friends and their young daughter, she wrote a long letter, begging Mario and Judy to reconsider their decision. The next morning she showed the letter to her husband, who also signed it. Bill and Deb then hand-delivered separate copies to Mario and Judy, at the same time inviting them to a marriage enrichment conference at their church.

Mario and Judy were a little taken aback at first, but they went to the conference and came away with a renewed commitment to work on their relationship. Not long after that, their daughter showed up at Bill and Deb's house, thanking them for saving her parents' marriage.

Fortunately, the Kindigs are not the only ones who have decided to intervene in a troubled marriage. In Washington, D.C., leaders from several major Christian groups have announced plans to recruit "back from the brink" couples (whose marriages nearly failed but didn't) to mentor other couples having marital difficulties. In Chattanooga, Tennessee, a nonprofit group called First Things First convinced local officials to require divorcing couples to attend a class detailing the effects of divorce upon children. In the first year, the classes resulted in a 19 percent decline in Chattanooga's divorce rate. And in California, another couple on the rocks received a letter from a concerned husband and wife with experience in these matters: Mario and Judy.

In 2001, a group of marriage experts issued a declaration, arguing that marriage is "not just a private affair of the heart" but also a public commitment between a man, a woman, and the wider society. With the release of such books as *The Case for Marriage* and *The Hidden Cost of Divorce,* couples are recognizing that divorce is not always an easy answer. "Every marriage waxes and wanes," says Linda Waite of the University of Chicago. "Getting divorced when things are awful is in some ways a shortsighted view. You're cutting off your foot because you have an ingrown toenail."[1]

No matter what sort of relationships populate your life—spouse, children, parents, friends, neighbors, and coworkers—try to do the unexpected thing, and give a touch of grace where it is needed.

Forgive when they hurt you.

Reach out when they withdraw.

Listen when they want to talk.

Most of all, love.

My friend, in those flashpoint moments of revelation, if we see others as Christ sees them, we will change the world—beginning with the people closest to us.

FLASHPOINT: TIME FOR A NEW ATTITUDE

Did you know that *Rocky,* the Oscar award-winning film, was the result of a flashpoint moment? On March 24, 1975, a struggling young actor named Sylvester Stallone witnessed a boxing match that changed his life forever. The championship bout between Muhammad Ali and Chuck Wepner was expected to last no more than three rounds, but Wepner, a young, virtually unknown boxer, proved himself astoundingly strong. As one round followed another and the underdog stayed on his feet, the crowd began to rally around him. Amazingly, Wepner lasted into the fifteenth round, eventually losing on a technical knockout.

Chuck Wepner's courageous loss inspired the twenty-eight-year-old Stallone, who wrote the *Rocky* screenplay in three days. The movie became a hit, then a series and a classic, and Sylvester Stallone discovered that he could write his own ticket in Hollywood. What more could he want out of life? Many things, as it turns out. Although he was a millionaire many times over, Stallone started to see his life in a different light. Why?

"I took a fierce emotional and moral inventory," he told

Parade magazine. "At that point, I said: 'I don't like this part of me. I do like that part.' In Column A, I had financial security. In Column B, I had nothing to elevate my emotions or my spirit. I literally tried a career upheaval. But there was a price to pay."

During the three years between *Cop Land,* a film for which he won critical acclaim, and *Get Carter,* a film that bombed at the box office, Stallone completed his personal inventory. "You never learn about yourself until you've been all the way down," he said. "When you've been pampered and protected and let other people think for you, you're going to eventually be at their mercy. When things start to go down, you can't expect them to rally. You have to do it for yourself. Maybe you'll win, maybe you won't. But if you don't fight back, you will never know what you're made of."

Stallone admitted that in his younger life he was arrogant, petty, and selfish. "When you're living in the fast lane," he said, "you tend to overlook the basic components that give your life meaning—relationships, getting to know someone really well, putting someone else first. People who are highly ambitious often don't focus on the needs of their immediate family, especially their children."

In 1985, his ten-year marriage fell apart under the pressures of sudden stardom. Years of partying and womanizing followed his divorce, including a short and disastrous marriage to actress Brigitte Nielsen.

But in 1997, Stallone decided to establish a solid and more mature personal life. He married Jennifer Flavin, and together they have two daughters.

"Now I understand what is sacred," said Stallone. "There

is nothing more exalting than requited love. . . . Real love is when you become selfless and you're more concerned about your mate's or your children's egos than your own. You're now a giver instead of a taker.

"I've been through the peaks and valleys," he said. "I understand now what is good for me. I can look at a goal and say, 'I've climbed that mountain, and it's not worth the climb.' Now, when a new mountain presents itself, I think: 'Is the pleasure worth the pain?'"

In the new light of his steadily burning passions of life and family, Stallone concluded with this: "I may not be at the top of my game with my career, but in my private life, I am."[2]

FLASHPOINT: A LIFE-CHANGING "CHANGE OF LIFE"

For fifty-two-year-old Dee Adams, "the change of life" became a life-changing event. Throughout her life, she has supported herself through a variety of jobs: apartment manager, cabdriver, baby-picture salesperson, and sign painter. As she approached menopause, a threshold experience that many women consider calamitous, Adams evaluated her life and discovered a new passion: cartooning. She soon developed a signature character named Minnie Pauz—a woman much like Adams herself.

For more than two decades, Adams had lived below the poverty line, but now she earns about $30,000 annually from Minnie Pauz, most of which comes from a pharmaceutical company that buys her cartoon for ads and featured spots at medical conventions. Adams is now planning to build a Minnie Pauz empire, branching out from her Web site (www.minniepauz.com) to gift books, greeting cards, mugs, calendars, and bumper stickers.

From her mobile home she creates a new cartoon each week and notifies her three thousand e-mail subscribers about the latest "Humor Replacement Therapy" update. She is currently seeking newspaper syndication, a challenging step she is tackling with the same determination that brought her this far.[3]

FLASHPOINT: CHOOSING FREEDOM

Tenth-grade dropout Gabriel Carrera was committed to his homeboys in the Latin Riders motorcycle gang. The son of Cuban refugees, Carrera was nicknamed "Crash" by fellow gang members because he'd been in seven separate motorcycle accidents that occurred, he says, "because I was drunk and stupid." His flashpoint experience started when someone stole his leather jacket. Determined to get it back, Carrera kicked in the door of the thief's apartment. A few moments later he found himself under arrest for breaking and entering.

Given a choice between prison and a Christian rehabilitation program, Carrera realized that his life of drug use and hanging with the gang had gotten him nothing but trouble. He chose the Christian rehab program. The threat of prison and the hopelessness of incarceration were the catalyst he needed to direct his passion away from drugs and toward God.

After graduating from the rehab program, he worked in Florida for a few years before attending Harvest Bible College in Ohio. Eventually, the school sent him to Cuba as a missionary. After his term of service, he returned to the United States and enrolled at the University of Hartford. Now in his late thirties, Carrera is a Pentecostal minister with a wife, a young son, and a degree in political science.[4]

FLASHPOINT: HITTING BOTTOM

Country music legend Merle Haggard has experienced several "hitting bottom" flashpoints. One of the first occurred when, at nineteen, he was sentenced to San Quentin Prison for up to fifteen years. "I stayed on closed security [solitary] for two years and turned twenty-one there," he told *Parade* magazine. "It wasn't where I wanted to be. I'd seen how big the system was. There was no hope. I opened my eyes, looked around, took in what's really expected of you in life versus what you thought as a child. It was a quick growing up. I charted a new course. I meant to stay out of prison."

After his flashpoint decision, Haggard became a model inmate and was paroled in 1960. After digging ditches and laying wire for a while, he began to get weekend jobs with bands and soon signed with a record company. By 1967, Merle Haggard was a bona fide country star.

Even stars can dim, however, and Haggard's life progressively took a downturn. He suffered from heart problems, married and divorced four wives, got into trouble with the IRS, and abused drugs and alcohol. Then, at another flashpoint, he pulled himself out of debt and put his life back on track. Today he is married to Theresa Lane, his fifth wife and the mother of his two young children, and he is grateful for how his life has turned out.

Haggard said, "Who would've thought that, at sixty-three years old, the most important thing in Merle Haggard's life would be a little family? . . . A lot of people—including me—had doubts about me surviving the money and heart problems, but I did. I've got to give credit to prayer. I'm happy and I'm thankful, and all of a sudden money's not the most important thing. The most important thing in my life is what my family feels about me. I never cared about that before."[5]

FLASHPOINT: I CAN BE MORE

Dr. Tony Evans remembers a flashpoint that affected his youth in a tremendous way—and the flashpoint was his father's. One night, he recalls, his father gathered the family around the kitchen table and told the children, including ten-year-old Tony, that he had given his life to Christ.

A few days later, Tony's father, a longshoreman from Baltimore, threw out all the liquor-making equipment in his basement. Tony's parents renewed their commitment to love, and the bickering between them grew quiet. Through times of Bible study and prayer, the entire family began to grow together. "Before, there was conflict, and suddenly there was peace," Evans told *World* magazine. "Our family became stable and strong."

His father's flashpoint deeply impressed Tony Evans, but so did the poverty surrounding his childhood neighborhood. To counteract the sense of "purposelessness" that plagued his inner-city friends, Tony committed himself as a young adult to helping others find their God-given purpose. After graduating from an all-black Bible college, Tony enrolled at Dallas Theological Seminary, at the urging of his professors.

Moving to the Deep South wasn't easy for Tony Evans. As only the third black man to enroll at the seminary, he had to attend white churches, and some of them were not very welcoming. Segregation was alive and well in Texas.

"As a child," said Evans, "I remember telling my father that I wanted a hamburger at the local White Castle restaurant, and then he told me we couldn't because they didn't serve blacks there. That's the first thing I remember as a boy that awakened me to segregation and racism. And then to later find out there were supposedly Bible-believing churches that did not integrate—that was especially confusing."

Rather than growing discouraged, Evans faced a flashpoint of his own: Instead of pursuing his ambition to become an evangelist like Billy Graham, he decided to be a church leader who would focus on uniting the races. To accomplish that task, he founded the Urban Alternative, a national nonprofit ministry that forges partnerships between suburban and inner-city church leaders to create Christ-based community renewal.

Fueled by this new passion, Evans invited ten people to discuss how they could start a church based upon biblical teaching and Christ-centered social reform. In stagnant, drug-infested south Dallas, the young man from Baltimore and his small circle of friends put together a plan.

The *Dallas Morning News* covered the event, but the reporter had her doubts about the significance of Evans's goal. "From a modest beginning of ten people, no church building, two pastors, and obviously limited resources," she wrote, "one wonders if there will be an Oak Cliff Bible Fellowship church in twenty years."

Don't you just love it when God proves the skeptics wrong? Tony Evans held that apartment meeting more than twenty years ago. Today the 6,000-member congregation is one of the nation's fastest-growing Bible churches—preaching life-changing salvation and working actively in social reform. Last year, according to a *World* magazine report, the church found jobs for 167 people and provided aid to 359 families through its community service programs. The world is still feeling the impact of Tony Evans's flashpoint decisions.[6]

FLASHPOINT: MULTIPLYING TALENTS

In 1995, at the age of twenty-seven, Lisa P. came to a flashpoint: She could no longer survive in a relationship with her abusive husband. Gathering her courage, she packed up her three children and left. To support herself and her kids, she took a job as an apartment manager in a rough neighborhood. One night she woke at 1:00 A.M. to find a man on top of her holding a knife to her throat. She managed to kick him away, but not before he cut her side and stomach. The next day, she went to the animal shelter and got the biggest dog she could find. Two weeks later, someone ran over her pet in the apartment parking lot.

Lisa packed up her kids again and left for a women's shelter. When her youngest son, then five, was diagnosed with developmental problems, social workers took him from her, breaking her heart. Lisa maintained custody of her other two children, but she received no child support from her husband, and she had to *pay* child support to the state for the son in foster care.

"Some of the social workers didn't think I'd make it," she told a reporter for the *Orange County Register*. "They said I would fail." To prove them wrong, she hunkered down, found a full-time job, began taking night classes, rented out a room in her apartment, and waited for God to provide. "This may sound funny," she said, "but when I'm in a really desperate situation I give God two days and he always comes through."

But wait. The story doesn't end there.

Meanwhile, across town from where Lisa lived, Pastor Denny Bellesi, who had experienced a flashpoint of his own, was trying to teach his congregation about the parable of the talents found in Matthew 25:14-15:

> AGAIN, THE KINGDOM OF HEAVEN CAN BE ILLUSTRATED BY THE STORY OF A MAN GOING ON A TRIP. HE CALLED TOGETHER HIS SERVANTS AND GAVE THEM MONEY TO INVEST FOR HIM WHILE HE WAS GONE. HE GAVE FIVE BAGS OF GOLD TO ONE, TWO BAGS OF GOLD TO ANOTHER, AND ONE BAG OF GOLD TO THE LAST—DIVIDING IT IN PROPORTION TO THEIR ABILITIES—AND THEN LEFT ON HIS TRIP.

One Sunday morning, Pastor Bellesi's passion for teaching compelled him to pass out $100 bills to the congregation. Leaving them with the money, he urged his church members to take the money and multiply it in Christ's name.

Terry Zwick received one of the bills and carried it with her through the week, explaining the lesson of the talents to those she met. Everyone she spoke to responded in some way, adding to her initial amount. By the end of the week she had collected $2,000. But who should receive the gift? Where would Jesus want her to invest it?

A friend nominated the perfect candidate—a classmate at the community college, a struggling single mom named Lisa. Terry invited Lisa to her home, asked her a few questions, and then sent her out into the night with a smile and a hug. A few days later, Terry and a few friends knocked on Lisa's door. In their hands they carried Christmas gifts for her children, an envelope with $1,000 in gift certificates, and a check for Lisa's January rent.

But wait. The story doesn't end there. Terry and her friends sat and talked with Lisa. They prayed for her. They virtually adopted her. Eventually, they decided to start a shelter for women in Lisa's situation.

Six weeks after receiving the $100 from Pastor Bellesi, Terri Zwick stood before the congregation and talked about her vision for the women's shelter, a place to be called Hope's House. She brought Lisa to the platform and explained how the initial $100 amount had been reinvested. You see, Lisa hadn't spent all the money she received on her own needs. She had given a financial gift to a single mother in the church choir and had purchased gifts for her daughter's Big Sister and her son's Big Brother.

That night, the vision of Hope's House became a reality. One man in the congregation went out and found a duplex that would work well as a shelter, then wrote a check for $75,000 as a down payment. Other men, inspired by his example, contributed an additional $15,000, and the church purchased the house.

But wait. The story doesn't end there. I want you to know about the flashpoint that started this whole process. It happened to Pastor Denny Bellesi more than ten years ago, and

I was privileged to witness it. At the time, I was on the founding elder board of the newly formed Coast Hills Community Church in Aliso Viejo, California. We labored each month to make ends meet while building and growing a healthy congregation.

While struggling to pay the bills at the church, some of the members became concerned about our outreach to other people. Even though we were essentially a missionary effort to south Orange County, some members felt that we should also send money to support missions elsewhere. Denny's view was that we should develop the church first, then send money to overseas missions.

One Sunday, Denny very quietly said to me, "I wish we didn't have to ask people for money. And when it comes to missions, I wish we could just hand money to people and ask them to use it to serve and minister."

Years passed, and I forgot about that conversation until one morning when I picked up the *Orange County Register* and saw Denny Bellesi on the front page. The photo showed him telling his congregation about his plan to hand out $100 bills, a unique idea that resulted in flashpoints for people throughout his congregation.[7]

FLASHPOINT:
TURNING GRIEF INTO GOOD

You may be familiar with John Walsh, who is regularly featured on the TV program *America's Most Wanted,* but you may have forgotten his story. On July 27, 1981, John and Reve Walsh were typical parents of a typical six-year-old, named Adam. Then, as Reve shopped at the Hollywood Mall in south Florida,

Adam disappeared—and the Walshes' lives changed forever.
Within hours of Adam's disappearance, John had set up a
command post in his home, where he helped the Hollywood
police search for his son. He printed 250,000 fliers. He posted a
$5,000 reward and then kept bumping it upward to keep inter-
est from flagging. He persuaded *Good Morning America* to do a
segment on Adam and other missing children.

Two weeks after Adam Walsh disappeared, his head was
found by a fisherman 120 miles away. Nothing else was ever
found, including the boy's killer.

"Along the path of grief," wrote Daniel De Vise, a
reporter for the Knight Ridder newspapers, "something transformed John Walsh into a Miltonian moral gladiator with a
superhero's sense of good and evil. He traces the change to a
conversation with the beleaguered Broward medical examiner,
Ronald Wright, who told him the horrors he had seen, the
glimpses of hell, and the sense of purpose that had kept him
sane. 'It's just that simple, John,' Wright told Walsh. 'There is
evil. And there is good.'"

After those flashpoints—the moment of his child's disappearance and the interview with the medical examiner—John
Walsh made a decision to fight crime. Over the past twenty
years, his efforts have changed our nation. At the time of
Adam's disappearance, there was no national clearinghouse for
missing children and very little coordination between police
departments. "It was much easier to locate a stolen car than it
was to locate a missing child," says Nancy McBride of the
National Center for Missing and Exploited Children.

Fifteen months after Adam's death, Congress passed the
Missing Children Act, which set up an FBI database of missing

children and empowered parents to report a case if local police refused. In February 1983, Walsh persuaded the FBI to adopt a new missing-children policy and take a more proactive role. In June 1984, the Walshes helped open the National Center for Missing and Exploited Children.

John Walsh's television program, *America's Most Wanted,* has led to the capture of 677 violent criminals. A television movie portraying Adam's story that ended with an interactive call for help from viewers resulted in the recovery of sixty-five missing kids.[8]

Sometimes, when you face the worst that life can throw at you, you have to work hard to make the pain yield to something better.

FLASHPOINT: A SECOND CHANCE

A few months ago I received the following e-mail from a man who read my book *Every Man's Battle,* a call for sexual purity:

> Dear Steve:
>
> On March 16, my sin came to light. Security at work came in and asked to see me. We went to a room, and they asked me if I had ever visited porn sites on the Internet. As ashamed as I was, I had to tell them yes. . . . They already knew, they even told me so. They asked about pornographic pictures on my computer, about my family, and even why I had Christian information and sinful things all on the same computer.
>
> The truth is, I had begun to look for a woman on

the Internet to become friends with and to have sex
with. I talked to many women and some sent me
pictures of themselves. I say all of this to let you
know it was *me* who made the choice to sin and no
one else. Even though I knew in my heart it was
wrong, I could not stop myself. Now the game I
played with God and myself came back into the light
and was staring me in the face.

On the way home, I started having chest pains
and I was desperate. How could I ever tell my
family? My church family? What had I done? Fear got
the best of me, and I thought I was having a heart
attack. I was rushed to the emergency room, and
I saw that the thought of losing me made my wife
cry. I was aching inside, wondering how could
I not hurt her anymore and tell her what I had
done?

I told her . . . [and] my wife was hurt, surprised,
and shocked.

I come to you today a humble and broken man.
A man who is very sorry and repentant for hurting
God, my family, myself, and my church family. In the
last nine months or so I had drifted away from God
and wondered why he was so far from me. Why did
he seem so distant? Where was he when I needed
him? Why did he let my father die? Why do I have
the feelings I do? None of it made any sense to me,
and I felt like I was being punished.

I have learned a lot of things since, and one of
them is that God was there all the time and I was the

one who had drifted away. I drifted of my own free will and bitterness. I refused to seek help for so long because of self—what would others think? What would they say?

Now we are going for marriage counseling, and I believe by God's grace our relationship can and will be restored. But on that day at work, Security escorted me out of the gate of my employer because I had been suspended without pay. My own sin nearly cost me my job and my family. I do not tell you this for pity but to show you that sin has consequences and I am paying the price.

The man who sent that e-mail came to a flashpoint where he decided to pray for a second chance—for God's Holy Spirit to burn away his sin and regret so he could begin his life anew.

Did you see yourself in any of the situations in this chapter? There are probably as many kinds of flashpoints as there are people in the world, because they spring from our past, our present, and our future—and only God can see all three clearly.

If you're feeling overwhelmed, hang on, dear friend. We're moving closer to the place where God can fire your heart with new purpose.

7

ARE YOU READY FOR A FLASHPOINT?

FAR BETTER IT IS TO DARE MIGHTY THINGS, TO WIN GLORIOUS TRIUMPHS, EVEN THOUGH CHECKERED BY FAILURE, THAN TO TAKE RANK WITH THOSE POOR SPIRITS WHO NEITHER ENJOY MUCH NOR SUFFER MUCH, BECAUSE THEY LIVE IN THE GRAY TWILIGHT THAT KNOWS NOT VICTORY NOR DEFEAT. —T. ROOSEVELT[1]

I CAN REMEMBER SITTING in my eleventh-grade American Literature class and reading Edwin Arlington Robinson's poem about Richard Cory. Remember this one?

> *Whenever Richard Cory went down town,*
> *We people on the pavement looked at him;*
> *He was a gentleman from sole to crown,*
> *Clean favored, and imperially slim.*
>   *And he was always quietly arrayed,*

And he was always human when he talked,
But still he fluttered pulses when he said
"Good morning"—and he glittered when he walked.
   And he was rich—yes, richer than a king—
And admirably schooled in every grace;
In fine, we thought that he was everything
To make us wish that we were in his place.
   So on we worked, and waited for the light,
And went without the meat, and cursed the bread,
And Richard Cory, one calm summer night,
Went home and put a bullet through his head.[2]

This startling poem was intended to jolt the reader. Why would a wealthy, attractive, educated person like Richard Cory commit suicide?

I'll tell you why—because Richard Cory never found a purpose for his life. Education and wealth and physical attractiveness are nice if one is fortunate enough to have been blessed with those qualities, but they do not bring personal fulfillment. If we want to fire our passion and find genuine joy in living, we're not going to look for it in such things. We have to look outside ourselves. Richard Cory never did.

But before we tackle where to look for our flashpoint inspiration, let's stop and evaluate where we are right now.

"Wait a minute," you might be saying, "I'm a long way from suicide. My life is basically okay, and I'm reasonably happy."

Congratulations. If you are perfectly satisfied with every aspect of your life and wouldn't change a single thing, well . . . maybe you're not ready for a flashpoint.

On the other hand, I don't know many people who don't

have at least one area of life they'd like to improve or change. Perhaps there's a problem you'd like to solve or a bad habit you'd like to get rid of. Maybe there's a relationship you'd like to mend, a dream you want to pursue, or a passion you'd like to explore.

WHAT WOULD YOU LIKE TO IMPROVE?

Perhaps you're concerned about your physical health—looking for the motivation and method to lose a few pounds. It's not easy, but it's possible. If you're like I was, the biggest barrier to losing weight is your belief that you are always going to be overweight. The change in my body did not occur until I changed my *mind*.

Want to better yourself intellectually? You may have never finished that degree—or even begun a study in an area that interests you. It's never too late to continue your education; life itself is a continual learning process.

My father did not graduate from college, because he enlisted in the navy after high school during the Korean War. When he finished his tour of duty, he moved home rather than go to college, because my grandfather convinced him that he should stay in Ranger, Texas, to manage the family's machine shop. So my father worked—but he never stopped learning. He met every sunrise with the attitude that he could learn something in the next twenty-four hours.

Over the years, my father became the best friend of bankers, researchers, and professors at Texas A&M University, even though he had only a high school education. Finally, in his late forties, he came to a flashpoint decision and stepped out to do what he had always wanted to do: He became a college student for the first time.

Want to improve your marriage? You can, you know. My wife, Sandy, will tell you that our marriage in the beginning wasn't everything a marriage is supposed to be. She might even say it wasn't *anything* a marriage is supposed to be. But she never gave up. She knew I had potential. She persevered through tough times, always believing that change was possible. Her attitude was that our marriage *could* be better and *should* be better. That attitude has kept our twenty-plus-year partnership on track, despite its share of ups and downs. Nowadays—and I say this for your encouragement, not to boast—our life together is mostly "up."

Want to change your attitude? You can. Many years ago, as the result of a flashpoint experience, I left a promiscuous lifestyle behind. I am amazed at how much of my life had centered on connecting with young women in any way I could. I wanted to be wanted. I felt lonely, and sometimes I only felt alive when I was involved in a sexual relationship.

But I was not alive, not really. I was slowly dying, without hope, promise, or dreams. Then my life changed in a flashpoint experience, and after that moment I knew life would never be the same. I met the Lord, and in him I found the anchor and the love I had been searching for.

Paul wrote that the love of Christ "is so great you will never fully understand it. Then you will be filled with the fullness of life and power that comes from God" (Ephesians 3:19).

I can testify to the power of that love. And so can those who knew me before and after my flashpoint with the Savior—some of whom openly questioned whether such a

drastic change could last. Today, after years of my growing
and maturing spiritually, those closest to me can attest that my
flashpoint experience with God changed me forever.
Life has never been the same, and it has never been better.

Want to improve your financial standing? Do you need
to pay off your debts, save more, or spend less? You can make
changes that will improve your effectiveness and efficiency.
When your life is in trouble, most likely your finances will be
also. That doesn't mean you won't have money. A lot of folks
like Richard Cory have plenty of it. But because of the way
they spend it, money becomes a cancer that eats away the core
of their lives.

I received my first credit card when I was in seminary. At
that time I was operating under the assumption that if I earned
$1,000 a month, I was entitled to spend $1,000 a month. When
the reality of taxes and Social Security hit and my cash flow fell
short of expenses, I made up for the difference with credit.

Have you seen that *I Love Lucy* episode where Ricky hires
an accountant to put Lucy on a budget? Lucy chafes under the
business manager's strict standards until she learns that she can
take grocery orders from her neighbors, accept their cash
payments, and leave the grocery bill for Ricky's penny-pinch-
ing accountant to settle at the end of the month. For a couple
of weeks she lives in high cotton, flashing a fist-sized wad of
bills, and Ricky thinks she has developed a sudden gift for
playing the stock market. Happy that his financial troubles are
over, Ricky dismisses the business manager, leaving Lucy with
a gigantic bill at the grocery store and a chagrined look on her
face.

My credit card and I got along famously until I discovered

that I could no longer make the minimum payment. For some reason, it had escaped my notice that I was digging myself deeper and deeper into debt. Even more amazing than my blossoming debt was the growing number of credit card offers arriving in my mailbox. Visa, MasterCard, Discover, American Express—*everyone* wanted to do business with me! I felt valued. I felt important. I was a dealer in high finance.

Ha! In reality I was a debtor in deep trouble. Some people pick up financial lessons easily; I've always been one who learns best from his mistakes. Finally, I had no choice but to change. I had come to the end of my ability to pay, so I took out a debt consolidation loan, which stretched out for so many years I could afford the monthly payment. Does this sound familiar? If so, you're ready for a flashpoint.

Want to meet new people and expand your horizons? You're ready for a flashpoint.

Want to grow closer to God? You're ready for a flashpoint.

Want to solve communication problems with a spouse, a family member, or a friend? You're ready for a flashpoint.

Want to improve your relationship with your kids? stretch your wings and try a new career? go back to school? study art or French or music or ballet? Do you have a trunkful of dreams that you've never pursued? Want to make a difference in the world? You're ready for a flashpoint.

Maybe you're a long way from feeling as desperate as Richard Cory, but the joy has fizzled out of your life, like helium escaping from a balloon. You want to soar, but right now you're just fluttering in the wind.

Take heart. You're not finished; you're just ready for a flashpoint.

EVIDENCE THAT YOU'RE READY FOR A FLASHPOINT

As I've spoken to callers seeking advice on the *New Life Live* radio program, I've discovered ten common signs that a person is ready for a flashpoint. Let's see if any of these fit your situation:

1. If nothing is ever quite good enough or you're never quite satisfied, you're ready for a flashpoint.
Ted Turner once said, "If I only had a little humility, I would be perfect."[3] He was joking—I think—but don't we all know people who are never quite satisfied because they can't attain perfection?

I've got good news for you! Perfection is unattainable, so you can rest from your efforts. Heed the word of the Lord, as spoken through the psalmist: "Cease striving and know that I am God; I will be exalted among the nations, I will be exalted in the earth" (Psalm 46:10, NASB).

Yes, excellence is a worthy offering, but perfection is nothing but per-fiction! You're not perfect, and neither is your spouse, your children, your boss, or your coworkers.

Not even your dog is perfect. So let it rest.

If you were to put a tape recorder in your pocket and record what you say to your family, friends, and colleagues, how much of it would come across as nagging?

Most perfectionists end up correcting the other person rather than connecting with the other person. The harder they strive and the more they demand, the less likely they are to ever experience a genuine relationship. If you're a perfectionist, you're likely to pass up more relationships than you could imagine because they will never be perfect.

If you're a perfectionist, you're living in a castle of fear, with "demands for perfection" as your defensive weapons. But here's the flashpoint: When you realize that perfectionism is nothing but an excuse to remain disconnected and remote from the vulnerability that comes with intimacy, then you can break free. Lay down your spears, tear down those walls, and step forward to discover that it's perfectly fine to be human in every area of life.

Through the prophet Hosea, God told his people, "I want you to be merciful; I don't want your sacrifices. I want you to know God; that's more important than burnt offerings" (6:6). Relationship is always more important than regulation, so stop trying to push yourself and the people in your life toward perfection. Give others the freedom to fly, and you'll find freedom yourself.

2. If it's easier to tell a little white lie than face the truth, you're ready for a flashpoint.
"That's not a lie," Alexander Haig once told a TV audience, "it's a terminological inexactitude."[4]

Do you find yourself backtracking or changing your mind because you didn't really think things through? Is it sometimes easier to fudge the truth than to deal with it? King Solomon, the wisest man who ever lived, tells us to "get the truth and don't ever sell it; also get wisdom, discipline, and discernment" (Proverbs 23:23).

Seek truth in your life. Only then can you be honest about the changes you need to make. All of us have blind spots, areas that we cannot see in ourselves but are obvious to others. Habitual lying, however, is a blind spot that can engulf your entire life.

My wife and I bought one of those TiVo gadgets that record television programs without the homeowner having to do anything. (The not-having-to-do-anything part was what drew me to the technology.) Thanks to our new gadget, when we lie in bed at night we can watch shows we would have missed without our TiVo.

I wish I could tell you that we prefer shows from PBS or the History Channel, but most nights we watch either Martha Stewart or Oprah Winfrey. One night my family and I watched Oprah interview a mother in prison who had shot her two children, killing one and paralyzing the other. The woman denied her guilt, and even my young daughter could tell that the convicted mother believed her own lies and excuses. Sandy and I took this opportunity to talk to our daughter about how easy it is to lie and then to believe your lies. "From that point," I told her, "it's only a matter of time until your entire life becomes a lie."

Godly character and deception cannot exist in the same soul. If you are caught in a web of deceit and lies, it's time for a flashpoint experience of truth.

3. If everyone around you never quite measures up, you're ready for a flashpoint.
To the Christians in Rome, Paul wrote: "You may be saying, 'What terrible people you have been talking about!' But you are just as bad, and you have no excuse! When you say they are wicked and should be punished, you are condemning yourself, for you do these very same things" (Romans 2:1).

If you've ever felt a rise of indignation as you read stories about people who had to hit the bottom before they reached out for God's help, you have fallen into the same trap as the Roman believers. A judgmental spirit can arise from pride, feelings of inferiority, or both.

A judgmental attitude is one of the most obvious signs that a person feels inferior. Tearing other people down can make us feel better about ourselves, but only for a little while. When we judge others, in effect we exalt ourselves (creating a false imitation of God) and wrongly assume the power to condemn. The Bible says, "God alone, who made the law, can rightly judge among us. He alone has the power to save or to destroy. So what right do you have to condemn your neighbor?" (James 4:12).

Instead of judging our friends and family, we are instructed to examine our own life. Paul added, "Don't condemn each other anymore. Decide instead to live in such a way that you will not put an obstacle in another Christian's path" (Romans 14:13).

If you have become the Judge Judy of your church or community, a flashpoint of humility can change your life!

4. If you're more apt to see the dark cloud than the silver lining or you live in fear of making a mistake, you're ready for a flashpoint. One day I had the privilege of visiting the office of Mary Kay Ash, founder of the Mary Kay cosmetics empire. It was a beautiful office, and it was quite . . . pink. I think the mirrors were pink. The carpets were pink. The curtains were pink. Everything was so pink that I got to thinking: When she fires someone they probably get a yellow slip rather than taint the color pink with a negative association.

I would like to have asked the woman who has created so

many millionaires, "What's up with the pink Cadillacs?" but she wasn't in that day. I enjoyed the opportunity to view her office, though, and as I turned to leave I spied a framed quote that must have been a key part of her success: "If you think you can, you can. And if you think you can't, you're right."

Do you worry too much? Are you afraid to cross an invisible boundary line that seems to shift from day to day? You don't have to live in fear. You can learn to live with confident abandon!

The prophet Isaiah wrote: "Do not fear anything except the Lord Almighty. He alone is the Holy One. If you fear him, you need fear nothing else" (8:13). Or, as Paul wrote to Timothy: "For God has not given us a spirit of fear and timidity, but of power, love, and self-discipline" (2 Timothy 1:7).

If you're determined to play it safe in life, then you're deciding that you no longer want to grow. Positive thinking alone will not conquer the world or change your life. But negative thinking can certainly make matters worse. If you dwell on what was or will never be rather than what is or what can be, then you are in need of a flashpoint experience.

5. If you can't remember the last time you had sheer silly fun, you're ready for a flashpoint.

When was the last time you laughed until your sides hurt? When was the last time you went out with your best friends and shared your heart? When was the last time you did something seriously silly? There is "a time to cry and a time to laugh. A time to grieve and a time to dance" (Ecclesiastes 3:4), but some people lose sight of the laughing and dancing.

Making time for fun in your life is not only a good idea, it's

113

a healthy idea! Wise Solomon wrote: "For the happy heart, life is a continual feast. . . . A cheerful heart is good medicine, but a broken spirit saps a person's strength" (Proverbs 15:15; 17:22).

Recently the New Life Ministries crew and about two hundred listeners took a Caribbean cruise. We had devotional gatherings, lecture meetings, and sessions where counselors answered questions, just like on the show. But do you know what had the greatest impact on our participants? Dancing.

Every night after the sessions were through, dinner completed, and our baked Alaskas snuffed out and stuffed down, we met as a group in the Crow's Nest. There, on a small parquet floor, we danced into the wee hours of the morning. When we studied the evaluations after the cruise, we noticed a recurrent theme:

"For the first time in my life, I danced."

"Thank you for getting me dancing again."

"I danced!"

"I missed dancing."

Dancing turned out to be the key to put many of our cruise participants in touch with fun. Some of them had not enjoyed such freedom in years. If you have forgotten how to play, you are ready for a flashpoint.

6. If your relationships have become strained or distant, you're ready for a flashpoint.
"Loneliness," wrote John Corry in the *New York Times,* "seems to have become the great American disease."[5]

How long has it been since you called your best friend (not your spouse) and invited him or her out to lunch? When was the last time you talked for an hour or longer to your parents or one of your siblings?

Friendships are essential nutrients for the human soul. Friends comfort and challenge us. "As iron sharpens iron," wrote Solomon, "a friend sharpens a friend" (Proverbs 27:17).

You cut yourself off from others at your own peril. You may not think you need friends today, but one day you will find yourself alone and in need.

A woman I know bought season tickets to the performing arts center in her town, thinking that she and her husband would enjoy several nights out during the year. But when the tickets arrived, she discovered they were all for Wednesday night performances, and her husband always had to work on Wednesday nights!

"I realized right then I had a problem," she said. "I work at home, and although I have a circle of friends on-line and through my business, I couldn't think of a single local friend to invite to the theater! That's when I knew my life had become unbalanced. I had all kinds of work-related friends but very few fun-friends."

Her solution? She immediately cleared Wednesday mornings to attend a Bible study with some women from church, and she tagged along with the group to lunch. In a matter of weeks she had renewed several old friendships, established several new ones, and as an extra benefit had more than enough friends to accompany her to the theater!

"Two people can accomplish more than twice as much as one," wrote Solomon; "they get a better return for their labor. If one person falls, the other can reach out and help. But people who are alone when they fall are in real trouble" (Ecclesiastes 4:9-10).

We need each other. If your friendships have grown distant, it's time for a flashpoint.

7. *If it's always someone else's fault, you're ready for a flashpoint.* The blame game is as old as Adam and Eve.

"I'm sorry I ate that fruit," Adam told the Lord. "But that woman you gave me—she made me do it!"

Eve had her own story, of course: "The serpent! It was all his fault!"

And so for thousands of years people have been ducking responsibility for their own wrongdoing and casting the blame on everyone else—including the devil. Well, friend, I'm sorry to have to tell you this, but Satan is not omnipresent, so most of the time we mess up on our own volition. As Christians, we are spiritual beings residing in a body of flesh (and still prone to fleshly failings), so refusing to take responsibility for our mistakes not only demonstrates a lack of character but a lack of maturity as well.

The prophet Jeremiah assured God's people that blame shifting was not allowed. "All people will die for their own sins—those who eat the sour grapes will be the ones whose mouths will pucker" (Jeremiah 31:30). Paul reinforced the teaching when he wrote to the believers in Galatia: "For we are each responsible for our own conduct" (Galatians 6:5).

Remember this: He who makes a mistake and fails to correct it makes another. Stand up to your mistakes and your sins. Confession is good for the soul. "People who cover over their sins will not prosper. But if they confess and forsake them, they will receive mercy" (Proverbs 28:13).

Please understand that sorrow about sin does not equal

repentance. A great many people are sorry for what they've done—when they get caught. Others may weep buckets of tears in genuine remorse, but if there is no desire to forsake the sin—to turn and go in a different direction—there is no repentance. If finger-pointing is your standard response, you're ready for a flashpoint.

8. If you never quite reach your goals or you're never quite satisfied with your results, you're ready for a flashpoint.
"Commit everything you do to the Lord," wrote the psalmist. "Trust him, and he will help you" (Psalm 37:5).

Timing is a big reason why many people cling to unfulfilled dreams and goals. Are you postponing your dreams in the hope that Aunt Gertie will leave you enough start-up capital in her will? Waiting to win the lottery? Waiting for the children to leave the nest, or until you lose thirty pounds, or your husband gets his act together? Are you telling yourself that you can't write a word until you can set aside three years to pen the Great American Novel?

If the Lord has placed a dream in your heart, don't wait for external events to grant you "permission." Don't allow yourself to be hampered by fear, but do take a look at your motives. Where did that dream originate?

If your goals and ambitions are to satisfy your pride, greed, or vanity, perhaps the thing holding you back is none other than the Spirit of God. Mark this down: The most important thing you can do with your dreams is examine them in the light of the Lord's will for your life. Cultivate the dreams that are born of the Spirit.

I honestly and fervently believe that we are the happiest

and most fulfilled when we are doing what God designed us to do. He knows our frame, he knows our talents, skills, and secret desires better than we know ourselves. If you pursue the dreams he plants in your heart, I can promise you'll find a more abundant life than you ever thought possible.

Don't waste your time chasing after the wrong things. If you "trust in the Lord with all your heart [and] do not depend on your own understanding," God will lead you. "Seek his will in all you do, and he will direct your paths" (Proverbs 3:5-6).

Notice that you are not to ignore your own understanding—God gave you a brain for a reason!—just don't solely depend on it. Rely on the Lord instead, and he will lead you to the dreams and goals that are in his plan for you.

9. If you're holding a grudge (be honest now), you're ready for a flashpoint.

"We do not squabble, fight, or have rows," says Irish writer Hugh Leonard. "We collect grudges. We're in an arms race, storing up warheads for the domestic Armageddon."[6]

Still angry with Cousin Joe for changing the channel the one time he baby-sat you? Are you harboring resentment because of something your sister said last summer, last year, or during your last pregnancy? Or maybe you're like the woman who got peeved with her fiancé when he made her pick up her own engagement ring from the jewelers, thus depriving her of the joy of having him slip it on her finger in a romantic moment. Granted, it was a bonehead move by the fiancé, but that was more than twenty years ago, and the wife still brings it up at every opportunity.

Booker T. Washington gave voice to a profound insight: Holding a grudge doesn't hurt the person against whom the grudge is held—it hurts the one who holds it. "I will permit no man," he said, "to narrow and degrade my soul by making me hate him."[7]

George Herbert wrote: "He that cannot forgive others breaks the bridge over which he himself must pass if he would ever reach heaven; for every one has need to be forgiven."[8]

The Bible tells us to "be kind to each other, tenderhearted, forgiving one another, just as God through Christ has forgiven you" (Ephesians 4:32). So when someone offends you—purposely or accidentally—forgive the offender and move on. Do not store up grudges like nuclear weapons. An arms race does nothing but prolong a cold war.

10. If you're frustrated or on "overload," you're ready for a flashpoint.

"Frustration is the wet nurse of violence," wrote David Abrahamsen in the *San Francisco Examiner* and *Chronicle*.[9]

If you find yourself weeping over a glass of spilled milk, a bad hair day, or one of those stains that magically appears in the washing part of the laundry routine, you're too tense. If you find yourself screaming like a banshee at your children, you're in sore need of a flashpoint, something to redirect your focus!

One woman told me about a flashpoint experience she encountered when her children were small. The toddlers, a boy and a girl, were only seventeen months apart, so they went through potty training together—a frustrating time for any mother.

"One day," she said, "while I was screaming out my frustrations at my kids, I happened to glance out the open window. The neighbor who lives behind me was in her backyard with her little girl, but she had looked up from the book she was reading to stare at my house with a shocked expression on her face.

"Suddenly, I heard myself through her ears and realized that I sounded like one of those crazy mothers I had always declared I would never be. From that day forward, I made myself a little rule—the more upset I became with my children, the more I would lower my voice. Screaming accomplished nothing and only frightened my kids. Speaking to them in a low, more intense voice told them I meant business and helped me keep my temper under control."

"It is better to be patient than powerful; it is better to have self-control than to conquer a city" (Proverbs 16:32).

Peace, my friend, is found in a person. And if you have a relationship with Jesus Christ, you have peace. Self-control is a fruit of the Spirit, so if you yield your life to the Spirit's gentle work, you will be able to rise above your frustrations.

DON'T SETTLE FOR LESS THAN THE BEST

If you saw yourself in any of the above descriptions, you're ready for your very own flashpoint experience. Decide right now to change your life! Don't be content with merely coping when you could be soaring above the things that now weigh you down.

Why settle for . . . *bitterness* when you could have *love?*

Why settle for . . . *detachment* when you could *connect* with other people?

Why settle for . . . *pettiness* when you could grow in *maturity?*

Why settle for . . . *self-absorption* when you could *help others?*

Why settle for . . . *compulsive performance* when you could have *grace?*

Why settle for . . . *scorekeeping* when you could have *mercy?*

Why settle for . . . *the way it used to be* when *today* has so much potential?

Why settle for . . . *the way it ought to be* when you could create a better *reality?*

Why settle for . . . *burdensome grudges* when you could experience the *freedom of forgiveness?*

Why settle for . . . *pride* when you could walk in *godly humility?*

Why settle for . . . *power* and *self-will* when you could learn the true power of *submission?*

Why settle for . . . *denial* when you could have *honesty* and *awareness?*

Why settle for less than the best that God has for you?

8

CAPTURING THE SPARK

WALT DISNEY'S ABILITY to creatively harness his flashpoint experiences is legendary. One of his signature moments occurred the day he had a bad experience at an amusement park. The seedy atmosphere, shoddy rides and attractions, inadequate bathrooms, and horrible food caused him to think as he left the park, *There has to be a better way.* On the heels of this *illumination* (stage one of a flashpoint experience) came *inspiration* (stage two): Why not develop an amusement park where the parents could have as much fun as the children? He pondered the idea, subjecting every element to a careful *evaluation* (stage three): Why not make each ride uniquely fun and interesting, serve good food, and make certain the facilities are spotless and well maintained? What would it take to make this park *the happiest place on earth?*

Evaluation led to *motivation* (stage four) when Disney turned his dreams into action by designing a fantasyland of fun and adventure. Long before Kevin Costner heard that mysterious voice whisper, "If you build it, they will come" in the movie *Field of Dreams,* Walt Disney believed that if he built a world of imagination, people would flock to it. When he encountered the inevitable obstacles, his *determination* (stage five) allowed him to overcome the odds and persevere. Finally, he experienced the *realization* (stage six) of his dream as thousands—and soon millions—of people thronged to Disneyland. With delight and great satisfaction, he heard the laughter of parents and children as they rode the spinning saucers, thundered down the slopes of the Matterhorn, savored delicious food, and traversed the park with smiles as wide as the Mississippi.

Walt Disney didn't simply create another amusement park. He built a place that reflected his passion, imagination, and inspiration. "Curiosity keeps us moving forward," he was fond of saying, "exploring, experimenting, opening new doors."[1] As a result, the Disney theme parks are like no other place on earth.

Walt Disney died before the completion of Disney World in Florida, but his widow was in Orlando the day they opened the gates. As the master of ceremonies introduced her and waved his hand across the blue sky, he said, "I wish Walt could have seen all of this."

Lifting her chin, Mrs. Disney looked out across the bustling park. "He did," she said simply.

CAN YOU ORCHESTRATE THE SPONTANEOUS?

If flashpoint moments are often unexpected and unplanned, how can we follow a "how-to plan" for creating a flashpoint experience? Simple: Open your eyes to the opportunities around you. I hope that as you've been reading this book you've been inspired by the stories and illustrations, and perhaps an idea has already occurred to you or taken root in your fertile imagination. If you are wondering how you can take that thought and use it to change your life, then you're at stage one of the flashpoint process. Read on.

FLASHPOINT STAGE ONE: ILLUMINATION

The first step of the flashpoint process—*illumination*—is almost self-explanatory: It's that moment when "the lightbulb goes on" and you suddenly see your life, your circumstances, or your opportunities "in a new light." In that instant, when you clutch a thought to your breast and savor it, you either recognize that something is not right or you realize you have an opportunity to create something better. Then, as you look around and see things as they are, ask yourself, *What if? Could I?* or *Why not?*

Walt Disney visited an amusement park and was inspired to build a better place. The illumination point for the Women of Faith conferences came as I sat in a success seminar and idly wondered why no one had thought to provide a similar event for Christian women. No doubt you've noticed that many of the flashpoint examples we've discussed stemmed from similar moments of illumination. Illumination occurs when you go through life with your eyes open, experiencing life and living in reality. You can't have an illumination experience if your mind is settled into ruts of worry or depression. Just as kindling must be dry and crisp in order for a spark to make it burn, your mind must be alert and open.

Don't go through life with false expectations. Learn to live with a sense of *expectancy*.

Elizabeth Barrett Browning once wrote: "Earth's crammed with heaven and every common bush afire with God; but only he who sees takes off his shoes. The rest sit round it, and pluck blackberries."[2]

"Expectancy," says Mark Buchanan, "is the belief that God will do something. Expectation insists He do it in just *this way*. Sometimes expectation blinds us more to the God who is here right now than outright disbelief does."[3]

When life comes to you clothed in routine and ordinariness, don't expect things to remain as they always have. Begin to look for new ways of doing things. Cultivate a sense of expectancy, and be prepared to see God work in ways you might never have imagined.

Take a moment to look at yourself and your surroundings. What season of life are you in? What unmet needs are there around you? What skills or talents do you possess that could help to meet those needs?

What is the status of your spiritual life? Would you say that you are diving into the life God planned for you or merely dog-paddling on the surface of all God has to offer?

What about your health and appearance? Are there things you could do to bring honor to yourself and your Creator? Do you have habits that need to be brought under control?

What about your social life? Do you have a strong circle of friends? Would your family say you are a joy to be around? Does your tendency toward anger make others tiptoe around you? Are you moody?

What about your mental life? Are you still learning and seeking out new ideas and new experiences? Are you reading books or do you "veg out" every night in front of the television?

If you are like most people, you have a tendency to protect your predictable world with denial. Human nature resists change. Because we like the status quo, we tell ourselves that things can't change or that we couldn't handle the pain of adjustment if the situation were altered. Instead of visualizing what we could do or be, we settle for what feels comfortable, even though "comfortable" may be destructive. We tell ourselves that everyone settles for less or that pain is just our lot in life. And in convincing ourselves of a lie, we remain in denial and never realize the full, creative, and satisfying life we are called to live.

Why do we so often miss the boat? Because we settle for second best. We grasp at flashy substitutes instead of taking hold of the genuine article.

I invite you to surrender all of your excuses today. Be honest with yourself, and recognize where and how you need to change, grow, improve, or surrender. Change is the essence of life—and it's worth the inconvenience, the difficulty, even the pain, because living is what God designed us to do.

Some of us will see that our life needs a change; others will have change forced upon them. But at the moment of illumination, if we seize upon an idea, we'll cross the threshold to the next stage: *inspiration.*

FLASHPOINT STAGE TWO: INSPIRATION

"You've got to have a dream," sang the island woman in Rodgers and Hammerstein's *South Pacific.* "If you don't have a dream, how ya gonna have a dream come true?"

If you want to make your flashpoint dreams come true,

you must first believe that dreams are possible. You need to believe that things can be different or that you can change.

Kate Krival, a successful speech pathologist in St. Petersburg, Florida, had one nagging annoyance in her life—an allergy to soap. Because the perfumes and artificial ingredients in most soaps aggravated her skin, she bought a book and taught herself how to make soap with all-natural ingredients. Her hobby became addictive, and after a few months of making soap, she gave up her $60,000 annual salary as a speech pathologist to make soap.

In order to raise money to begin her business, Kate's Soap, she sold her house, borrowed $5,000 from her brother, cashed in her retirement plan, and eliminated luxuries such as her cell phone and cable TV.

Everybody thought she was crazy, but after Breck Fleming of CNBC interviewed her for a segment on the *Business People* cable television program, he said, "We saw a woman who quit her job, is doing something that she loves, is enjoying it and doing quite well."[4]

For now, Kate Krival is happy . . . making soap. She believed in her dreams and is well on her way to making them come true.

The word *inspiration* comes from a Latin word meaning "to blow" or "breathe upon." I love this word picture because I can just see the Spirit of God "blowing" an idea into my brain. I truly believe that many, if not most, of the best ideas in my life have been God-breathed.

At your flashpoint moment, when the illuminating idea first enters your brain, open your mind and embrace the opportunity. Start by clarifying the vision: Picture yourself doing or being what you'd like to do or be. Visualize what you want to accomplish. For example, what would you be able to wear if you lost twenty pounds? What would that empty house across town look like as a homeless shelter? Can you see yourself serving as a "hugger" in the Special Olympics? What comes to *your* mind as you ponder the possibilities?

Collect news stories about people who are doing something similar to your idea. Create a "flashpoint" bulletin board with pictures and headlines that inspire you. Prepare yourself to move ahead. See the way life could be, and dream of the day when you will live differently—marching to the beat of a different drummer.

Don't ask, "What's in it for me?"

Try asking, "What's in *me* for it?"

Remember this: Nothing is impossible with God! Do not let others confuse, contradict, or confound you. Galatians 5:1 reminds us that in Christ, we are completely free to follow his plan for our life: "So Christ has really set us free. Now make sure that you stay free, and don't get tied up again in slavery."

To the new Christians in Rome, Paul wrote: "Don't copy the behavior and customs of this world, but let God transform you into a new person by changing the way you think. Then you will know what God wants you to do, and you will know how good and pleasing and perfect his will really is" (Romans 12:2).

The inspiration stage is all about freeing your mind and heart to dream about what God would have you do. His will really is good and pleasing and perfect—and, like a loving parent, he wants both to bless you and mature you! So seek his face, and let your heart dream.

When I was growing up, and until he died, my father never failed to tell me he was proud of me. He let me know I could probably do anything I set my mind to. I know many parents say that to their kids, but I believe Dad was sincere about it. The confidence he instilled in me set me free to go through life asking, "What's the big idea?"

If you don't look for the big idea, you are missing moments of inspiration that could change your life. Big ideas are how thoughts become events, how concepts become buildings, how questions become answers.

What's the "big idea" of your life? What were you put on earth to do? Raise children? That's wonderful! Raise great kids with all the creativity you can. But if part of your mission is to raise great kids and you are spending most of your life at the office, I suggest you resign, change jobs, or find a new career.

Maybe the "big idea" of your life is to serve others, but you often find yourself working alone and for yourself. Something's wrong with that picture! You need to do whatever it takes to get out of your solitary existence and into the lives of the people God intended for you to serve.

The next time you find yourself doing something new, fun, or exciting, look around and ask yourself this potentially life-changing question: *What's the big idea?*

The big idea just may be the inspired flashpoint for which you were designed.

FLASHPOINT STAGE THREE: EVALUATION

Sometimes when I get excited about a big idea or a new insight, I am disappointed to find out that I am not the first one to discover that particular hill of opportunity. That's okay. Often all it means is that the tools or procedures required to meet the need already exist.

After illumination and inspiration, *evaluation* is the next step in following through on a flashpoint experience. God wants us to use our intellect and our skills to analyze the task we're undertaking. Scripture says, "Let us test and examine our ways" (Lamentations 3:40), and the prophet Isaiah wrote, "'Come now, let us argue this out,' says the Lord" (Isaiah 1:18). The most important part of the evaluation process is determining whether your flashpoint idea is in line with God's will for your life.

"Now wait a minute, Steve," you might protest, "how can you say that I should consider my flashpoint in light of God's will when you have filled this book with examples of people who did things without even *thinking* about God?"

Point well taken. Flashpoints are not confined to the Christian experience; nor, as we've mentioned before, do they always point a person toward good. Anyone can have a flashpoint experience and decide to move toward good *or* evil. But if you have committed your life to the Lord Jesus Christ, he wants you to offer your dreams to him and wait until he gives you a peace before proceeding. "Seek his will in all you do, and he will direct your paths" (Proverbs 3:6).

That's not to say that if we commit our flashpoints to the Lord everything will come off without a hitch. In the real world, things are rarely that simple. God's plan for us may involve suffering (which matures and refines us), hardship (which teaches us to endure), and sacrifice (through which we learn how to discern true worth from perceived value). Still,

God is not afraid of our questions or even our doubts. He loves us, and he has given us a promise. "'For I know the plans I have for you,' says the Lord. 'They are plans for good and not for disaster, to give you a future and a hope'" (Jeremiah 29:11). His plan for us is ultimately good, and it will lead us to a divinely ordained future and hope.

The evaluation stage is not the time or place to give in to your fears; it is a time for sound reasoning and thorough research. What is it going to take to bring your dreams to life? Have other people ever tackled this problem? What were their methods and results? Is anyone else trying to do what you'd like to do? Can you join forces, or should you work on your own?

The evaluation stage is also the point at which we assess—and change, if necessary—our attitude about our dreams and desires. Let's suppose our goal is to become more physically fit in the coming year. Instead of seeing the steps toward that goal as "have to" experiences, we should visualize them as "choose to" opportunities. Instead of dragging ourselves out of bed because we *have to* walk a mile to stay healthy, we should get up thinking, "I *choose to* walk today because I *choose to* be healthier than I was last year."

Operating under a "have to" mind-set is like driving a car with one foot on the gas and one foot on the brake. Nobody likes feeling trapped, and human nature naturally resents confinement. But if we see our work, our options, and our goals as choices we can freely (and happily!) make, the steps toward the goal will become completely enjoyable.

As part of a "choose to" mind-set, we must be open to learning new things. When we think we know everything—

or even enough—about a certain subject, we tend to listen to new ideas with boredom or even cynicism. But if we will visualize ourselves as eager students, we'll be open to new ideas—and we might be surprised by what we learn! A mind that expands to embrace a new idea never returns to its original dimension. A friend of mine puts it this way: The quickest way to become an old dog is to stop learning new tricks.[5]

After we've researched our options and have begun our evaluation, it's time to construct a plan. I received the following letter from a woman who had attended one of our Gentle Eating seminars. After the conference, she didn't do anything drastic, but she constructed a plan that involved small deviations from her past patterns. Eventually, those small changes made a big difference in her life.

> Dear Steve:
>
> We attended the November 1994 seminar, and I still review the literature and my notes from time to time to keep on track.
>
> We're eating less fat, and I am walking three days a week with a lady from our church. At first I could only handle a half hour, but now we walk for an hour most days. I have arthritis in my knees, but they seem to be getting better.
>
> The changes we have made in our lifestyle have been small steps one at a time, but each one has become permanent, and I have lost sixteen pounds over the past year. The weight has come off so slowly that I didn't notice it until most of my clothes started feeling loose. I'm not focusing on the scales or weight

loss but rather on eating healthy and staying fit regardless of my weight, which coincidentally seems to be coming down.

The most liberating thought I took away from the seminar was from you—when you told us that people like us with slow metabolisms cannot eat like our thin relatives who have metabolisms running in high gear. Suddenly my inferiority feelings were gone as I realized these "skinnies" are not more disciplined or together than I am. And I also realized they are as likely to die prematurely of stroke or heart disease as I am if they don't learn what I'm learning now. Poor Ted, my tall, slim husband, eating ice cream by the bucket, had a stroke two years ago, but thanks to the seminar, he now realizes that fat kills and is making the same life changes I am.

Remember this, friends: It is more important to know where you're going than to get there fast.[6]

Bible scholars estimate that when Moses led the children of Israel out of Egypt, he was taking responsibility for more than 3 million people plus their livestock. According to an army quartermaster, Moses would have required 1,500 tons of food each day to feed so many people. If they could have hauled that amount of food in railroad boxcars, a single day's provisions would have required two freight trains, each a mile long, to bring in the supplies, not including the firewood for cooking. The children of Israel would have needed 4,000 tons of fuel per day to cook their food.

The Israelites also required water. For drinking and washing a few dishes, their forty-year journey in the wilderness would have required 11 million gallons per day.

Do you think Moses stopped to figure out all these details before he left Egypt? I doubt it, though the size of the task might have been one of the reasons he hesitated back at the burning bush! Although there is value in planning, when God gives a command, he supplies the necessary resources. Moses obeyed in faith, and God supplied his people with water and food. Manna rained down upon the children of Israel so they did not starve. Their sandals and clothing did not wear out during the entire forty-year sojourn in the wilderness (Deuteronomy 8:3; 29:5).

So if you're thinking God can't possibly handle the vexing details that arise in your life, think again! "And this same God who takes care of me will supply all your needs from his glorious riches, which have been given to us in Christ Jesus" (Philippians 4:19).

At age seventy-four, writer Tad Szulc was informed that he had incurable cancer. Over the years of his life, he had already survived a plane crash, open-heart surgery, and a previous bout with cancer, but never before had he heard a doctor say that his condition was *incurable*.

"Surprisingly," he wrote in an article in *Parade* magazine, "as the doctor's words sank in, I did not feel fear or panic. Nor did I feel sorry for myself. In fact, after the first shock, I felt a curious sense of calm. In a strange sort of way, I said to myself, 'Okay, I guess it is fated.'"

Szulc decided to spend his remaining lifetime being medically treated so he could live as long and as well as possible. He traveled, spent time with his family, and learned about his disease, colorectal cancer. And he said, "My advice to fellow cancer patients is this: Try to develop a good disposition to help the mind prevail over matter. Don't feel sorry for yourself. Lead as normal a life as possible. Do not miss regular treatments. Keep in touch with your oncologist. If you are religious-minded, put your faith in prayer. I myself believe in prayer and have been very grateful to all those who have called to say they were praying for me. Above all, be positive. Myself, I opt for optimism."[7]

When life throws you a curveball, remember you're not alone on the field. God is with you, and he will support and guide you even through the valley of the shadow of death.

As you research and evaluate your plan, look around and identify possible supporters. Even Jesus didn't go it alone—he called twelve disciples. Who will support you in your project? Who might oppose you? Can you turn the naysayers into supporters by somehow involving them in your efforts?

At one of his flashpoints, Michael Stewartt, a private pilot, visualized pilots flying reporters and politicians over forestland endangered by clear-cutting and pollution. Today his organization, Lighthawk, has enlisted 150 volunteer pilots who provide fast support to people who need to see the devastation of our forestlands for themselves.[8]

Ranya Kelly, a housewife in Arvada, Colorado, discovered that local stores were throwing away new shoes simply because they had minor imperfections or were no longer in style. When she salvaged the shoes from dumpsters to donate to homeless shelters, she was threatened with arrest—because the material in the dumpsters technically belonged to the hauling company! So she spoke to the manager of the hauling company, who was happy to give her permission to take whatever she wanted from the dumpsters.

Because Ranya Kelly chose to find a way around the obstacle in her path by turning a possible foe into an ally, her salvage effort grew into an organization, the Redistribution Center, which now supplies thousands of dollars worth of clothing items to the needy each day.[9]

So . . . if you think your husband will try to sabotage your diet, encourage him to walk with you! If your children need you at home with them, find a way to work out of your kitchen, den, or garage. If you need money to finance a missions trip to Peru, ask your church's missions committee if it would prayerfully consider supporting your venture.

The other day I heard a story about an ancient king who wanted to test his people. He had a boulder placed in the middle of a well-traveled road and then hid himself in the nearby brush to see if anyone would have enough initiative to remove the huge stone.

Some of the king's wealthiest merchants and courtiers came by and simply walked around the boulder. Many loudly blamed the king for not keeping the roads clear.

When the king's strongest warriors and knights approached the stone, they cursed it and struck at it, but in the end they wheeled their mounts around the rock and whacked their way through the underbrush.

Then a peasant came along, bowed beneath a load of vegetables. Upon approaching the rock, the peasant lowered his burden and tried to move the stone to the side of the road. After much pushing and straining, he finally succeeded. Only then did he notice a flat pouch lying in the center of the road—

way. The pouch contained gold coins and a note from the king, indicating that the money was a reward intended for the resourceful person who managed to remove the stone from the road.

The peasant learned a lesson that many of us never quite grasp: Every obstacle presents an opportunity to improve our condition.

Don't curse or grumble about the obstacles in your path—find a way to move them, or pray your way through! Call to mind the words of Booker T. Washington, who said, "I have learned that success is to be measured not so much by the position that one has reached in life as by the obstacles which he has overcome while trying to succeed."[10]

Don't be afraid to ask for help. People are surprisingly generous with advice, especially if you take the time to befriend them first. And remember to be thankful. You may meet a mentor who will encourage and support you for years to come!

Keep your eyes open. Don't take things at face value. Look. Think. Examine. Question. Don't just smell the roses—discover what makes them so fragrant. A careful and thorough evaluation will often lead to even greater opportunities.

Don't give up when you encounter bumps in the road. Remember, when you're traveling up a mountain, it's the bumps you climb on!

9

GIVING WINGS TO YOUR DREAMS

WHAT IS THE GREATEST IDEA you've ever had? Did you do something about it? I used to think that great ideas and big concepts were the most valuable things in the world, but now I realize they are practically worthless. That is to say that great ideas and big concepts are worthless *unless* you are motivated to do something about them.

Novelist Angela Hunt, who collaborated with me on the writing of this book, says that people are always coming up to her with ideas for novels. "I thank them politely," she says, "but ideas are really a dime a dozen. Scads of them pop into my head all day long. But what makes a story good is the *execution* of that one truly golden idea that resonates within your soul. You've got to have passion for a story, and it has to come from deep inside your heart."

FLASHPOINT STAGE FOUR: MOTIVATION

Once you've been inspired by your big idea and you've made your plans, done your research, and enlisted allies, there will come a moment when you are ready to take the first step. But no matter how much planning and preparation you've done, sometimes the first step is difficult . . . and frightening.

Angela Hunt says that the first draft is always the hardest part of writing a novel. "First I get the vision for a book," she says, "and I'm usually able to sell it on the strength of my enthusiasm for the project. After I've signed a contract, I schedule the book project on my calendar. When it's time to begin, I spend a couple of weeks doing research, planning my writing schedule, sketching an outline, drafting character descriptions, and sending letters to people who might help answer questions. If I'm not careful, though, I could spend an entire month doing background work, none of which is going to put the first word on the page."

At some point, like a swimmer teetering on the edge of a diving board, we all have to take a deep breath and jump in.

Motivation is all about taking that first leap into cold water or that first step in the race, to use one of my favorite analogies. Don't get so caught up and comfortable in the preparatory stages that you never step out and actually begin to do the work. To paraphrase Confucius, the race of a thousand miles begins with a single step, and at some point you have to lace up your shoes and *start running.*

Why is that first step so hard? Usually it's because at some level you have convinced yourself that you have to run the race alone. No matter how many people are cheering you on, sometimes you can't hear their voices—but, inevitably, the catcalls of fear, doubt, and insecurity echo in your ears.

You worry that your work won't measure up to your vision.

You worry that your strength won't last until the job is done.

You worry that the result won't be worth the effort and your supporters will be disappointed.

When fear, self-doubt, and insecurity rear their ugly heads, rest in this truth: If God has called you to this work, he will supply what you need. He is faithful, he is powerful, he is the consummate provider. "For since the world began, no ear has heard, and no eye has seen a God like you, who works for those who wait for him!" (Isaiah 64:4).

The *why* behind your journey determines how long you will last in the race. If you're running just to get by or to produce "just enough," you'll quit as soon as that goal is reached. But if you're running to change your world, you may be in the race for the rest of your life! Your motive determines your motivation.

The apostle Paul wrote: "All athletes practice strict self-control. They do it to win a prize that will fade away, but we do it for an eternal prize. So I run straight to the goal with purpose in every step" (1 Corinthians 9:25-26).

What happens if you lose your motivation? Anyone who has supervised other people knows that some folks work for a while, but then they lose their focus and don't seem motivated to work, improve, or even show up. People who lose motivation need to be reminded of the reason they are working. If your flashpoint idea is running out of steam, it's probably time for a new flashpoint.

What motivates you? I hope it's not just pride, a desire for prominence, or simply to make a lot of money. There is more to life than self-aggrandizement, fame, or gold. There are people who need what you have—weak people who need your strength, blind people who need your insight, captives who need to be set free.

Are you motivated? If not, do whatever it takes to repair and reenergize your drive to make a difference. Making a splash and making a difference are two very different things.

Suze Orman, the author of several best-selling money management books, didn't start out as a financial expert. Her first job was as a waitress at a diner called the Buttercup Bakery. There, she says, "I . . . learned how important it is to take pride in life's little accomplishments. When I helped out in the kitchen, nothing made me feel better than putting two eggs on the grill, flipping them over easy, and serving them just the way the customer wanted."

While working at the Buttercup Bakery, Orman began to dream of opening her own restaurant. She asked her parents for a loan, but they didn't have the money. The next day at work, one of her regular customers noticed her downcast look. When he asked what was wrong, she said, "Fred, I know I can do more if somebody would just have faith in me."

The next day, Fred handed her several checks totaling $50,000, along with a note that said, "The only collateral on this loan is my trust in your honesty as a person. Good people with a dream should have the opportunity to make that dream come true."

Motivated by Fred's faith in her, Suze Orman took the checks to Merrill Lynch, opened an investment account, and continued making her plans. But her investments soured, and she lost the money. Wondering about the vagaries of the stock market, she decided to investigate becoming a broker. She applied at Merrill Lynch, was hired, and worked her way up the ladder, learning all the while. Eventually, she repaid Fred and her other patrons, with interest.

Shortly after repaying the note, she received a thank-you note from Fred, who had used the money she sent to pay medical bills. "That loan may have been one of the best investments I will ever make," he wrote. "Who else could have invested in a 'counter girl' with a million-dollar personality and watched that investment mature into a very successful career woman?"[1]

God wants to invest in you. Through his prophet Isaiah, God told his people, "But now, O Israel, the Lord who created you says: 'Do not be afraid, for I have ransomed you. I have called you by name; you are mine'" (Isaiah 43:1).

God also calls *you* by name. He loves *you,* and he has a special plan for your life. The apostle Paul assures us "that God, who began the good work within you, will continue his work until it is finally finished on that day when Christ Jesus comes back again" (Philippians 1:6).

What greater motivation could we need? If the vision resulting from your flashpoint is in agreement with the will of God for your life, he will uphold and support you until the dream is reality! Press on!

FLASHPOINT STAGE FIVE: DETERMINATION

Success is not like winning the lottery—a little risk, one lucky announcement, and it's all over but the shouting. No, after setting your dreams into motion, you will face challenges and have to overcome obstacles. Count on it. And when trouble arises, you must be determined to push ahead when everything within you tells you to turn around, give up, or quit. Dreams do come true, but the dreamers who see the fruition of their dreams are those who have the determination to stay in the race from start to finish, through good times and especially through bad.

Once you've taken the leap into the race, carry your dreams and desires like a precious bundle, persevering toward the goal even when all looks hopeless. Motivate yourself with phrases like "I won't stop, even if . . ." and "I must make a difference because . . ."

Once you've reached the *determination* stage, goal setting will make a tremendous difference in your efforts. Instead of striving for a huge payoff at some far-off finish line, try setting closer, more manageable goals. Reaching these intermediate goals will give you a sense of satisfaction and stoke the inner fire you'll need to remain in the race for the long run.

Don Wallace is a believer in setting goals with determination. Now the president and CEO of the highest-selling recreational vehicle dealership in the United States, he's been setting goals, writing them down, and meeting them since he was eight years old.

Wallace says that when he started setting goals, he would write, "I am going to do something by this date," and then he'd save up his money or begin to work on his goal. Usually, he accomplished it.

When he was a teenager, his goals included buying a Honda motorcycle, a 1966 Chevy II Super Sport, marrying soon after high school, and owning a house by age eighteen.

He achieved all those goals, even though he'd be the first to admit he wasn't the smartest kid in his class—though maybe the most determined.

After trying his hand at farming, Wallace sold a trailer for $500 dollars. He used that money to buy a bigger trailer, which he also sold. Then he bought another trailer and sold it as well. With every sale he made a profit, and soon he was selling trailers full-time. Eventually he came to a flashpoint and realized that recreational vehicles might sell better than trailers in Florida. After all, many of the local residents were retired, and with time and money to spare.

When Wallace began his RV business, he ordered a set of motivational tapes that urged him to write down his five-year goals. One of his goals, he recalls, was to save $200,000 so he could retire and never have to work again. Time passed, and his business flourished, reaching sales of $90 million by 1989. But that same year, Wallace's brother died in a car accident, bringing Wallace to another flashpoint.

When he was offered a substantial sum for his business, which would have allowed him to meet his retirement goal, Wallace had to ask himself: *What do I really want?*

The answer, he soon realized, was to stay in the race. He loved his company, his employees, and his customers. So he kept the dealership. Ten years later, he sold the business to a private, employee-owned equity firm, with the stipulation that he remain as president and chief executive. If he accomplishes his latest company goals, Wallace, now in his early fifties, will be doing what he loves for as long as he's able, and Lazydays RV SuperCenter will double its annual sales to reach one billion dollars by 2005. "Ain't no *if* about it," he says.[2]

As you run the race, avoid the pitfall of complaining. Grumbling and grousing only churn the air, accomplishing nothing.

I don't know why it's so human to complain, even when we're doing what we love to do. We complain when it's sunny because we need rain; when it rains, we complain because it's not sunny. We might as well face the truth that we need sunshine and rain, good and bad, success and failure to become mature, well-adjusted adults. Runners who are training for a marathon run on sand, asphalt, and along the side of the road. They run uphill, downhill, and across flat terrain, because they never know what they'll encounter in the race. Likewise, as we run toward our goals, we can be certain to encounter bad times and good, so we may as well consider our burdens a blessing.

According to Scripture, complainers are often prone to bragging: "These people are grumblers and complainers, doing whatever evil they feel like. They are loudmouthed braggarts, and they flatter others to get favors in return" (Jude 1:16).

Why do complaints and bragging pour from the same mouth? Richard Allestree, a seventeenth-century pastor, said we shouldn't be surprised to find such faults combined, since they are streams issuing from the same fountain:

> The very same pride that prompts people to boast about themselves and overvalue what they are also presses them to condemn and despise what they have. As long as they measure their good by that inflated idea they have formed of themselves, they necessarily think what they have is below them. . . .
>
> But the worst and most unhappy instance of all is

in our behavior toward God. We dispute His distribution of gifts with the same boldness—or even greater—with which we disparage others. What else could be meant by our impatient murmurings over things that are immediately governed by Providence? . . .

Thus when we rail against the wickedness of one person, the deceit of another, for impoverishing us; when we angrily blame our defamed reputation on the malice of those who malign us, and our disappointments on the treachery or negligence of our friends; we are actually concluding either that there is no overruling Providence who could have prevented those events, or else (which is equally horrid) we accuse God of not having done well in permitting them. . . . In this way we can rightly estimate the danger of our discontent. Though at first introduced by the inordinate love of ourselves, it is apt to culminate in hatred and blasphemies against God.[3]

David Lloyd George, a British statesman who served as prime minister during World War I, an economic crisis, and the rise in Ireland of the Sinn Fein movement, was asked how he remained in good spirits through the nation's many difficulties. He replied, "Well, I find a change of nuisances is as good as a vacation."[4] I love that unbridled optimism!

Someone once told me that "success is not getting what you want, but wanting what you get." So, my friend, if you find yourself tempted to complain about a situation, consider the source of such sin . . . and ask yourself if you wouldn't be better off thanking God for the change of nuisances in your life!

A young woman once came into the kitchen where her father was reading the newspaper at the table. Sinking into a chair across from him, she began to flood the room with a stream of complaints—her college professors were too strict, her boyfriend wasn't dependable, and she had no idea what God wanted her to do with her life.

Without a word, her father stood, walked to the sink, and filled three pots with water. The young woman watched, confused, as her father put the three pots on the stove and turned up the heat beneath each container. As the pots came to a boil, he gathered items from the pantry and refrigerator.

Into the first pot, he dropped a handful of carrots.

Into the second pot, he slid a raw egg.

Into the third pot, he sprinkled a handful of ground coffee.

After a few moments, he crossed his arms and turned to his daughter. With a smile, he inclined his head toward the stove. "Come here, honey, and tell me what you see."

His daughter rose and looked into the pots. "Okay," she said, staring at the food tumbling in the boiling water. "What's the point, Dad?"

Her father reached for a spoon and scooped out a few bits of carrot. "These were hard when I put them into the water," he said, "but now they're soft."

"And the egg," his daughter said, following his thoughts, "was soft when you put it in, but now it's hard boiled."

Her father nodded. "Exactly."

"But what about the coffee?" She pointed to the last pot. "It hasn't changed."

"No, it hasn't. But it turned plain water into something

fragrant and delicious." Grinning, he reached for a coffee mug. "Want a cup?"

Ah, my friend, there's a powerful lesson in that simple illustration. Are you like a carrot, hard and snappish until you go limp in the heat of adversity? Perhaps you're more like an egg, which begins with a soft heart but hardens under testing. Outside, you may look exactly the same, but something on the inside has toughened.

Or perhaps you're like the coffee . . . in the heat of a stressful situation, you color your surroundings with fragrance and flavor.

The next time life turns up the heat, ask yourself: Am I behaving like a carrot, an egg, or a measure of coffee?

To succeed with determination, you must resist the temptation to complain and overcome the distress of discouragement. Even Jesus felt the need for rest, and on several occasions he was beleaguered by disappointment. But with each fresh sunrise he rose and reapplied himself to his task.

David, the psalmist, knew about discouragement, doubt, and misgivings. He wrote: "When doubts filled my mind, your comfort gave me renewed hope and cheer" (Psalm 94:19).

When you find yourself feeling stressed and doubtful, go to the quiet place where you meet with God and let him speak to you. Don't spend the time rattling off your complaints—God knows your grievances and discouragements. Instead, sit in silence, lift your thoughts toward the Father, and let him speak to your heart. He will comfort and encourage you—if you will take time to listen.

Clint Black, the country singer who has sold more than 16

million albums, began his working life as a newspaper solicitor, selling subscriptions to the *Houston Post* from door to door. The job wasn't easy, and the prospective customers weren't always nice. Says Black, "One time, a man slammed his door in my face and screamed, 'I don't want no . . . paper.' I forced myself to knock again and was able to tell him how great the paper was. I ended up selling him a subscription. I was soon among the top subscription sellers, and, like other successful salesmen, was given responsibility for training newcomers."

During those years, Black began playing the harmonica and guitar. At eighteen, he turned his attention to becoming a professional musician, and no matter how long and hard the struggle, he never stopped pressing toward his goal. "I never lost sight of my dreams," he says. "I'm sure my perseverance came from what I learned knocking on strangers' doors."[5]

Satan would like nothing better than to weigh you down with discouragement, and you must be wary of that particular hindrance. To encourage the new believers in Asia, Paul wrote: "So don't get tired of doing what is good. Don't get discouraged and give up, for we will reap a harvest of blessing at the appropriate time" (Galatians 6:9).

Jesus said, "I have told you all this so that you may have peace in me. Here on earth you will have many trials and sorrows. But take heart, because I have overcome the world" (John 16:33).

Remember—unless *within* us there is that which is *above* us, we shall soon yield to that which is *about* us.

If giving up was hard, no one would do it. But giving up is easy, procrastination is easy, and it's easy to be distracted. At any time you could look around and see others who are running faster, doing more, finding more success, making more money, winning more people to Christ.

Don't compare yourself to others! You are on a special God-designed path, following his plan for *your* life. Don't take your eyes off the one who is charting your course. Remain steady, keep running, and persevere in his plan for you. Don't give up. No one ever said the race would be easy, but the outcome will be worth it.

"Therefore, since we are surrounded by such a huge crowd of witnesses to the life of faith, let us *strip off* every weight that *slows us down,* especially the sin that so easily hinders our progress. And let us run with endurance the race that God has set before us" (Hebrews 12:1, italics added).

Do you see the italicized phrases above? Once you have begun a project, do not allow trivial, unimportant things to distract your attention. Set boundaries (because you have to allow time for important relationships), and focus when you are within those boundaries.

What are some of the things that distract you from your goals today? It may be something as trivial as e-mail, the telephone, the gorgeous weather outside, or a jagged fingernail you can't seem to ignore. In situations like these the answer will be found in devising a workable schedule that will reward your accomplishments with free time to enjoy the many other opportunities that life presents.

Distractions also come in the form of issues that seem important, such as your compassions, compulsions, companions, or consumptions. Learn how to balance each area of life within the framework of what God has called you to do. Rather than thinking of your priorities as a ladder with God on the first rung, family on the second, and work on the third, think of your life as a wheel. Each spoke of the wheel represents some aspect of your life—your hobbies, your relationships, your charities, your dreams—but, as a Christian, the entire wheel is devoted to God. At any moment of the day, one section of the wheel will be uppermost, but that's okay, as long as the wheel is kept in balance.

Contemporary life offers its own share of distractions. How long has it been since you sat in a completely quiet room? If you're like most people, it has probably been a long time. The media continually distract us. We work with the radio blaring; we turn on the television the moment we walk through the door; we even shop to music playing throughout the mall. The discipline of silence is rarely practiced these days, but often it is in silence that we best hear the still, small voice of God. You may need to consider setting aside one spoke of your wheel for quiet reflection and meditation.

After a flashpoint, you will be running toward a goal, and you may find new goals behind every short-term finish line. Great! Keep going! Run the race with diligence and with an eye toward new opportunities, but do not allow yourself to be distracted from your primary purpose. Adopt new goals only if they lie beyond or on the same path as your primary goal. Leave the rabbit trails to the rabbits.

Determination may require you to develop resilience in the face of adversity. When things go wrong—and sometimes they will—you have to hold tight to your goals. Here's how:

1. *Communicate effectively.* Determine what went wrong, and see if you can discover the reason why. Do not cast blame;

simply state the facts—and then find a way to prevent the error from recurring.

2. *Keep calm.* Don't overreact. When talking to your associates, friends, and coworkers, take care to avoid loaded words like *always* and *never.* Instead of saying, "You always forget to write things down," try saying, "What would help you remember to write things down?"

3. *React in a timely manner, but don't rush to judgment.* Gather all the facts before you draw conclusions and rush to fix the problem.

4. *Keep the problem in perspective.* Try to imagine how the situation could be worse—and then look for the bright lining in the cloud. Yes, there was a problem, but didn't you learn something from it? As long as you're living, there's still hope. Try not to let emotion cloud your image of how bad the situation is—it will probably look better in the light of a new day.[6]

Finally, determination may require you to raise your level of competence. Don't set out to write the Great American Novel without studying the form and taking a few writing classes. Don't set out to be the next Lucille Ball without honing the finer skills of comedy. Make an effort to get the right tools— planning carefully, if necessary, so you can afford them.

You won't win the race on a whim. Champions often make the winning look easy, but we rarely see the depths of preparation and the hours of practice they have invested. Walt Disney once said, "People often ask me if I know the secret of success and if I could tell others how to make their dreams come true. My answer is . . . you do it by working."[7]

We all know people whose homes are filled with

half-finished projects that were begun with every good intention and left by the side of the easy chair. If you want to persevere in your flashpoint decision and reach your goal, you'll have to work for it. But you won't be working alone.

One of my favorite stories involves a man, a stone, and God. In a dream, God told the man to go outside and push against a huge boulder in his front yard. So every morning for the next few weeks, the man went outside and strained against the rock. He pushed and groaned and prodded and shoved, but the rock never budged.

Finally, in a fit of exasperation the man fell to his knees and lifted his eyes to heaven. "What were you thinking, Lord?" he cried, wiping sweat from his brow. "You told me to push this rock, and I've been pushing for weeks, yet it has not moved an inch!"

A voice from heaven rumbled among the clouds, then whispered in the man's ear. "I told you to push the stone," God said, "I didn't tell you to *move* it. I'm the only one who can move it, and when you're ready, I will. By the way, look at your hands."

The man looked at his hands. They had grown callused and tough with the work, and his arms bulged with muscles. Though his efforts had seemed fruitless, he had grown strong; and now he was beginning to grow wise.

Sometimes God wants us to learn a lesson through our labor and struggle. He wants us to push against the obstacles and grow patient and strong until he is ready to move the boulder. When we are ready for him to do the impossible, he will!

As a wise man once said, there is a difference between

perseverance and obstinacy—one is a strong *will* and the other a strong *won't*.[8]

One thing I know for sure: When there is a wide gap between expectation and reality, misery exists in between. If you are expecting your days to be easy and hassle-free, you are going to be disappointed. *Life is difficult.* It is difficult in different ways for different people, but the bottom line is the same. You can never make enough money to avoid financial trouble, and you can never develop enough character to avoid heartbreak. These things are part of life. If you accept life's difficulties without giving in to them, you'll have a better chance of pursuing your dreams with realistic determination.

Wake up each morning asking God to see you through the day's rough moments. He promises to wipe our tears away, not prevent them. Weep when the tears come, but don't give up.

If a project is worth pursuing, it will require initiative, energy, and endurance. One stroke could not chisel Michelangelo's David. One page does not create a great novel—one draft won't even do it. You must persevere and see the project through.

FLASHPOINT STAGE SIX: REALIZATION

When someone asks me to autograph a book, I usually write the reference for my "life verse"—Ephesians 3:20—below my name. I love the promise it contains: "Now glory be to God! By his mighty power at work within us, he is able to accomplish infinitely more than we would ever dare to ask or hope."

Paul wrote: "And I am sure that God, who began the good work within you, will continue his work until it is finally finished on that day when Christ Jesus comes back again" (Philippians 1:6). I love this verse as well because it reminds me that we are not "finished," not even when we reach our goals. Even in stage six, when our dreams are realized, our life purpose is not yet complete.

I've often heard parents say, "We're upset because our children didn't turn out the way we hoped they would." Well, are they in heaven? Because if they aren't, they're still turning out! We all are!

Once we've seen our God-ordained flashpoint goals become a reality, it's time to look around. There's bound to be another goal around the next corner. As long as we're alive, we are meant to be in the race.

"What? You've got to be kidding! I thought I'd be able to rest when I reached the finish line!"

You won't need to rest . . . if, along the way, you've taken the time to renew yourself daily through prayer and meditation upon the Word of God.

Daily renewal is important. David wrote: "It is useless for you to work so hard from early morning until late at night, anxiously working for food to eat; for God gives rest to his loved ones" (Psalm 127:2). Physical rest is crucial; it is impossible to function properly without sleep.

According to the Sleep Foundation, more than 60 percent of Americans get less than the eight hours of nightly rest the average adult requires, compared to less than 50 percent in 1960. Worse, 43 percent report being too sleepy to perform efficiently at work or at home a few days a month or more.[9]

As important as physical rest is, spiritual rest, or renewal, is crucial, too. You should cultivate the daily habit of spending time with God. Paul wrote: "That is why we never give up. Though our bodies are dying, our spirits are being renewed every day" (2 Corinthians 4:16). Even though our physical bodies weaken a little every day, our spirits are renewed through communion with God.

The prophet Isaiah wrote many things about the need for resting in the Lord. He told the people of Israel, "The Sovereign Lord, the Holy One of Israel, says, 'Only in returning to me and waiting for me will you be saved. In quietness and confidence is your strength'" (Isaiah 30:15).

In Isaiah 40:31, we find one of the most beautiful pictures of how resting in the Lord upholds us:

> BUT THOSE WHO WAIT ON THE LORD WILL FIND NEW STRENGTH.
> THEY WILL FLY HIGH ON WINGS LIKE EAGLES. THEY WILL RUN
> AND NOT GROW WEARY. THEY WILL WALK AND NOT FAINT.

Now let me paraphrase this verse in light of our flashpoints discussion:

> If we will wait patiently and look to the Lord, we will find power, strength, and vigor for the task. We will soar with new dreams and new goals. We will remain in the race, and we will not tire. We will endure even when the race forces us to slow to a walk.

Jeffrey Turner, a Florida dentist, is now waiting on God, because God waited on him. As a high school student in Kentucky, Turner felt God calling him to be a pastor. But the young Turner wasn't willing to listen. "Security, money, success," he said at age forty-two. "I wanted those things like anyone else."

So he pursued them. After completing his education, he built a successful dental practice in south Tampa, establishing a base of more than 2,300 patients. He and his wife, Susie, lived with their four children in a large and comfortable house.

But in 1999, Turner came to a flashpoint experience and knew he would no longer be content as a dentist. Something inside nagged at him, and he had to admit that he lacked a passion for his vocation.

"When I told Susie about this feeling, she was completely supportive," he told a reporter for the *Tampa Tribune*. "She knew it was coming before I did. My parents and in-laws were the ones who were concerned."

After much prayer, Turner put his dental practice on the market. "I decided to put it in God's hands," he said. "I was in no hurry."

But an offer came quickly. And Turner found himself enrolling in seminary, a three-year commitment. He enrolled at Southern Baptist Seminary in Louisville at the same time his seventeen-year-old son headed off to college. He plans to maintain his dental license, and he's not ruling out the possibility that God may want him to use his medical expertise on a mission field somewhere.

"It's funny," he said. "I know I've been called, but I don't know what or where. Again, I will leave that to God."[10]

The value of a realized dream can never be underestimated. Do you recall the wonder you felt when you were finally able to drive out of the driveway by yourself? Do you remember the goose bumps that prickled your arm when you signed papers and bought your first house? Living the dream of a lifetime is far more exciting than driving or owning. Don't stop working until the dream God gave you becomes the reality you present to the world.

"But, Steve, I keep working and working, but I never see any results!"

Let me tell just one more story about the realization of dreams:

The Chinese bamboo tree is one of the most remarkable plants on earth. Once the gardener plants the seed, he will see nothing but a single shoot coming out of the bulb—for five full years! That tiny shoot, however, must have daily food and water. During all the time the gardener is caring for the plant, the exterior shoot will grow less than an inch.

At the end of five years, however, the Chinese bamboo will perform an incredible feat. It will grow an amazing ninety feet tall in only ninety days! Now ask yourself this: When did the tree actually grow? During the first five years, or during those last ninety days?

The answer lies in the unseen part of the tree, the underground root system. During the first five years, the fibrous root structure spreads deep and wide in the earth, preparing to support the incredible heights the tree will eventually reach.

You may be like a Chinese bamboo, my friend. You may be working and dreaming and planning and persevering, yet you feel as if God is taking forever to flower your dream into any visible result.

Wait patiently on the Lord. You are growing, even if the growth is underground, hidden deep in your character. In due time, God will reveal everything he's grown in you. Those who wait on the Lord will never be put to shame.

10

FLASHPOINT BARRIERS

WHY DOESN'T EVERYONE experience the thrill of a flashpoint moment and the fulfillment of their goals? Because some people never make it into the race. Others stare at their flashpoint vision and never believe in it. Still others enter the race, but they come to a hurdle and never even attempt to leap over it. They stop, dead in their tracks, blocked from victory by a barrier that shouldn't have even been on the course.

There are three emotional barriers that will prevent you from acting effectively on your flashpoint experience: fear, guilt, and anger.

CONQUER YOUR FEARS

Fear comes in many packages, including fear of failure, fear of humiliation, fear of rejection, and fear of the unknown. When Eugene Louis Jean Joseph Napoleon, also known as the

"Prince Imperial," was a young boy, he would stand brave and unflinching while the soldiers fired off their cannons, yet he seemed afraid of the nearby ocean. Determined to help the child overcome his fears, one of the royal attendants picked the boy up and tossed him into the waves. After struggling onto dry land, the young prince ran away shrieking in terror.

Later, after he had been caught and comforted, someone asked why he was afraid of the sea and not the loud cannonade of the soldiers. The little boy considered the question for a moment, then answered, "Because I'm in command of the soldiers, but I'm not in command of the sea."[1]

Aren't we just like that little boy? We aren't afraid of the things we can control, but the unknown can make us as jumpy as kittens. Not even David, the warrior king, was immune to fear. In Psalm 55:5, he wrote: "Fear and trembling overwhelm me. I can't stop shaking."

Norman Vincent Peale once wrote, "Fear can infect us early in life until eventually it cuts a deep groove of apprehension in all our thinking. To counteract it, let faith, hope and courage enter your thinking. Fear is strong, but faith is stronger yet."[2] A mature love for Christ knows no fear. The apostle John wrote: "Such love has no fear because perfect love expels all fear. If we are afraid, it is for fear of judgment, and this shows that his love has not been perfected in us" (1 John 4:18).

Let's look at some of the more common varieties of fear and learn how to overcome them.

Persistent Pessimism

A recent edition of the *New York Times* featured news of a new toy—a plush "Ask Me More Eeyore," modeled after the gloomy character from A. A. Milne's *Winnie the Pooh*. The

Ask Me More Eeyore, manufactured by Fisher-Price, is designed for children ages three to seven. The *Times* remarked that these are "just the right ages, apparently, to learn about undaunted pessimism."

Instead of giggling, like many stuffed animals on the market, this one responds to questions in a dreary, dubious voice. When you squeeze his left front leg, he says, "Go ahead. Ask a question. If you want."

His twenty random responses include, "Don't count on it," "Doesn't look good," "Outcome looks sort of gloomy," "You can't win them all," "Looks good for you. Must be nice," and "I'd tell you if I knew. But I don't."

And sometimes Eeyore will ask the child a question: "You wouldn't want me for a friend, would you?"

Sigh. As if life isn't tough enough for some kids.[3]

Do you have a gloomy Eeyore in your life? Perhaps you've taken on that role for yourself! Most of us don't need help trying to find the cloud behind the silver lining—it's the first thing we see! But if we're too busy looking for all the things that can go wrong, we often miss the blessings God has prepared for us.

So the next time you're tempted to pronounce a glass half-empty, think of Noah, who began to build an ark when there wasn't a cloud in the sky; or David, who picked up a tiny stone without regard for Goliath's spear, shield, and sword. Those men had faith, the kind of resolute confidence that overcomes the clouds of pessimism and shines as bright as the noonday sun.

All-Encompassing Anxiety

When Lord Mountbatten, the British naval commander, was five years old, he did not like going to bed in the dark. "It

163

isn't the dark," he confided to his father, "there are wolves up there."

His father smiled. "There are no wolves in this house, Son."

"I daresay there aren't," answered the precocious little boy. "But I *think* there are."[4]

Oh, the beasts and monsters our brains can conjure up! Even though our rational brains *know* there are no wolves in the attic or monsters under the bed, still we lie awake at night with all our fingers and toes tucked beneath the blanket.

God never intended for us to live a life of worry. Like a protective father, his Spirit indwells us while his angels watch over us. Nothing can happen to us unless it is part of his sovereign plan for our life, and we've already seen that his plan for us is good, designed to give us hope and a future.

"Why worry?" Walt Disney once asked. "If you've done the very best you can, worrying won't make it any better."[5]

A believer full of worry is like an eagle with iron boots. The footwear may fit and even look good, but it will prevent the eagle from ever discovering the joy of soaring in flight.

Jesus said it this way:

> I TELL YOU, DON'T WORRY ABOUT EVERYDAY LIFE—WHETHER YOU HAVE ENOUGH FOOD, DRINK, AND CLOTHES. DOESN'T LIFE CONSIST OF MORE THAN FOOD AND CLOTHING? LOOK AT THE BIRDS. THEY DON'T NEED TO PLANT OR HARVEST OR PUT FOOD IN BARNS BECAUSE YOUR HEAVENLY FATHER FEEDS THEM. AND YOU ARE FAR MORE VALUABLE TO HIM THAN THEY ARE. CAN ALL YOUR WORRIES ADD A SINGLE MOMENT TO YOUR LIFE? OF COURSE NOT. AND WHY WORRY ABOUT YOUR CLOTHES? LOOK AT THE LILIES

AND HOW THEY GROW. THEY DON'T WORK OR MAKE THEIR
CLOTHING, YET SOLOMON IN ALL HIS GLORY WAS NOT DRESSED AS
BEAUTIFULLY AS THEY ARE. AND IF GOD CARES SO WONDERFULLY
FOR FLOWERS THAT ARE HERE TODAY AND GONE TOMORROW,
WON'T HE MORE SURELY CARE FOR YOU? YOU HAVE SO LITTLE
FAITH!

SO DON'T WORRY ABOUT HAVING ENOUGH FOOD OR DRINK
OR CLOTHING. WHY BE LIKE THE PAGANS WHO ARE SO DEEPLY
CONCERNED ABOUT THESE THINGS? YOUR HEAVENLY FATHER
ALREADY KNOWS ALL YOUR NEEDS, AND HE WILL GIVE YOU ALL
YOU NEED FROM DAY TO DAY IF YOU LIVE FOR HIM AND MAKE THE
KINGDOM OF GOD YOUR PRIMARY CONCERN.

SO DON'T WORRY ABOUT TOMORROW, FOR TOMORROW WILL
BRING ITS OWN WORRIES. TODAY'S TROUBLE IS ENOUGH FOR
TODAY. MATTHEW 6:25-34

Do you ever listen to classical music in your car? There are days
when I have been beaten up so badly at work that all I want
to do is roll up the windows on the drive home and listen
to something that will soothe my soul—Mozart, maybe, or
Beethoven. But classical music is so pure, so clean and precise,
that its loveliness is marred whenever I drive under a utility wire
and a burst of static fills my car. When I listen to the rock music
from my youth, I can barely hear the static under the pounding
drums, wailing guitars, and screaming lyrics. But when I put on
the quality stuff—well, violins just don't sound their best when
the radio waves hiss and crackle with static.

Worry is soul static. You are not going to enjoy God's

peace if worry comes crackling through to irritate and agitate your frame of mind. You will never know the meaning of joy if fear broadcasts static into your heart.

Worry is highly overrated. Despite your well-meaning mother's admonitions ("Wear clean underwear! You just might end up in the emergency room!"), you don't have to live as if disaster looms over every day of your life. Banish worry's grip on your heart by fortifying your life with courage, trust, faith, hope, and vulnerability.

If you believe that God has led you to a flashpoint decision, don't worry about things that can't be helped. People who cross their bridges before they come to them have to pay the toll twice! Plan as much as you're able, and then leave the rest to God.

Debilitating Phobias

During World War I, a French colonel disciplined a young officer for showing fear in battle. When the commander, Ferdinand Foch, heard about the incident, he rebuked the colonel, not the officer. "None but a coward," he said, "dares to boast that he has never known fear."[6]

A few weeks ago, I was watching an early morning talk show when an actress confessed her fear of flying, then said she had to travel to Europe to work on a film. "Are you flying?" asked the host.

"Yes," she answered, "and I'm going to get plastered on the flight over so I'll be too drunk to be afraid." How sad, yet true, for many people.

The current list of phobias is almost comical (for example, arachibutyrophobia is the fear of peanut butter sticking to the roof of one's mouth), but there's nothing funny about fear for the folks who suffer from genuine phobias. According to some estimates, 50 million Americans suffer from some kind of extreme fear. The majority of phobia sufferers are women— from 55 percent for social phobias up to 90 percent for specific phobias such as agoraphobia (fear of public places).[7]

Fortunately, researchers are making tremendous progress in determining the nature of phobias and how they can be treated. Exposure therapies are helping psychologists stamp out phobias, while new drugs, such as Paxil, are working within the brain to snuff out the spark of a phobia before it bursts into flame.

The good news is that exposure therapy can be successful in eradicating most phobias. The problem is that so few people seek help; most prefer trying to avoid the thing that awakens terror within them. Phobias can wear out their sufferers because the feelings they generate seem so real. But most of the time, the perceived danger is a neurochemical lie—and the lie should be exposed. "Your instincts tell you to escape or avoid," says psychologist Steven Phillipson, clinical director of the Center for Cognitive-Behavioral Psychotherapy in New York City, "but what you really need to do is face down the fear."[8]

My friend Patsy Clairmont, once a sufferer of agoraphobia who could not leave her house, now travels nearly every weekend. Rather than stay at home in her safe cocoon of predictability, she drives to the airport, boards a plane, and then stands to speak all alone on a stage before thousands of women who've come to participate in a Women of Faith weekend. Patsy is a shining example of how much you can do once you overcome your fears.

All of Patsy's fears were unrealistic. The chances of her falling in her bathroom, hitting her head on the toilet, and dying in a household accident were greater than her chances of dying in a plane crash or looking silly in front of 20,000 women. Because she's such an exceptional speaker, the true tragedy of her life would have been remaining housebound by fear instead of venturing into the wide world.

What made the difference for her? Jesus Christ. After accepting Christ, Patsy gradually turned over all the hidden parts of her life to the Lord, including her fears. And now she is no longer afraid.

Jean Toomer once wrote: "Fear is a noose that binds until it strangles."[9] Don't let fear cut off your opportunity for a rich and meaningful life. Seek help today, and know that God is whispering, "Don't be afraid, for I am with you. Do not be dismayed, for I am your God. I will strengthen you. I will help you. I will uphold you with my victorious right hand" (Isaiah 41:10).

BANISH YOUR GUILT

The second most common barrier to flashpoint victories is guilt. Guilt produces feelings of unworthiness and shame, blocks our mobility and freedom, drains our creativity, silences our voice, and sabotages our success and innovation.

It's important that you understand this fundamental truth: All of us have sinned, and sin produces guilt. Romans 3:23 tells us that "all have sinned; all fall short of God's glorious standard." No one is perfect; only Jesus lived a perfect life.

Guilt does serve a useful purpose. It reminds us that we have done wrong, that we have done something that serves our selfishness instead of serving God. Someone once said that conscience is what hurts when everything else feels good, and that's true. Sin can be fun, but Hebrews 11:25 refers to the "fleeting pleasures of sin."

Sin is like a serpent with a deadly bite. And when we're feeling the pain, we can become depressed. Sometimes we feel so burdened that we become convinced that God can't forgive us and he can't use us. And so we never enter the race, never push forward to our flashpoint victory. We may catch a glimpse of life as it could be lived, but the dark clouds of guilt close in and crowd out all hope of the future.

David, the king known as "a man after God's own heart," was no stranger to guilt. You may recall the story of how he saw a beautiful woman, Bathsheba, bathing on the rooftop of her house. Being the king, he sent for her, slept with her, and sent her home. When Bathsheba, whose husband was away at war, sent word that she was pregnant, David had the man transferred to the front lines, thus ensuring his death.

David managed to evade his guilt until the prophet Nathan arrived at the palace and delivered a word from the Lord. "You are the man!" Nathan roared, pointing a gnarly finger at the king. "You have done a terrible thing!"

David's heart knocked within him as he realized the truth. Yes, guilt can serve a purpose. It reveals the chasm between God's holiness and our own corrupt sinfulness.

After days of sorrow, David poured out his confession in a psalm of prayer:

HAVE MERCY ON ME, O GOD,

BECAUSE OF YOUR UNFAILING LOVE.

BECAUSE OF YOUR GREAT COMPASSION,

blot out the stain of my sins.

WASH ME CLEAN FROM MY GUILT.

PURIFY ME FROM MY SIN.

FOR I RECOGNIZE MY SHAMEFUL DEEDS—

THEY HAUNT ME DAY AND NIGHT.

AGAINST YOU, AND YOU ALONE, HAVE I SINNED;

I HAVE DONE WHAT IS EVIL IN YOUR SIGHT.

YOU WILL BE PROVED RIGHT IN WHAT YOU SAY,

AND YOUR JUDGMENT AGAINST ME IS JUST.

FOR I WAS BORN A SINNER—

YES, FROM THE MOMENT MY MOTHER CONCEIVED ME.

BUT YOU DESIRE HONESTY FROM THE HEART,

SO YOU CAN TEACH ME TO BE WISE IN MY INMOST BEING.

PURIFY ME FROM MY SINS, AND I WILL BE CLEAN;

WASH ME, AND I WILL BE WHITER THAN SNOW.

OH, GIVE ME BACK MY JOY AGAIN;

YOU HAVE BROKEN ME—

NOW LET ME REJOICE.

DON'T KEEP LOOKING AT MY SINS.

REMOVE THE STAIN OF MY GUILT.

CREATE IN ME A CLEAN HEART, O GOD.

RENEW A RIGHT SPIRIT WITHIN ME.

DO NOT BANISH ME FROM YOUR PRESENCE,

AND DON'T TAKE YOUR HOLY SPIRIT FROM ME.

RESTORE TO ME AGAIN THE JOY OF YOUR SALVATION,

AND MAKE ME WILLING TO OBEY YOU.

THEN I WILL TEACH YOUR WAYS TO SINNERS,

AND THEY WILL RETURN TO YOU.

FORGIVE ME FOR SHEDDING BLOOD, O GOD WHO SAVES;

THEN I WILL JOYFULLY SING OF YOUR FORGIVENESS.

UNSEAL MY LIPS, O LORD,

THAT I MAY PRAISE YOU.

YOU WOULD NOT BE PLEASED WITH SACRIFICES,

OR I WOULD BRING THEM.

IF I BROUGHT YOU A BURNT OFFERING,

YOU WOULD NOT ACCEPT IT.

THE SACRIFICE YOU WANT IS A BROKEN SPIRIT.

A BROKEN AND REPENTANT HEART, O GOD,

YOU WILL NOT DESPISE.   PSALM 51:1-17

Notice that David didn't attempt to cast blame, rationalize his actions, or excuse his wrongdoing. Instead, he laid his sin out before the Lord. David owned it, and then he cast it off. He prayed for forgiveness, then acknowledged—through faith—the coming joy of a restored relationship with God.

Perhaps you, like David, have been haunted by sins in your past. I don't know what your past holds, but if you're like most people, you have your fair share of guilt, shame, regrets, resentments, and bitterness. When you try to put the past behind you, these voices cry out, *How dare you move on without us? You have to take us with you, and you'll never be all you could be with us in your life.*

In *The Peaceable Kingdom,* Stanley Hauerwas writes:

> Our first task is not to forgive, but to learn to be the forgiven. Too often to be ready to forgive is a way of exerting control over another. We fear accepting forgiveness from another because such a gift makes us powerless, and we fear the loss of control involved. . . . Only by learning to accept God's forgiveness as we see it in the life and death of Jesus can we acquire the power that comes from learning to give up control.[10]

You must be willing to be forgiven. You must be willing to admit that you need forgiveness and that you need it from the person you have wronged. Sometimes that person is a loved one, a neighbor, or even a stranger. Often the one we have wronged is God.

Many people struggle with guilt even after they have confessed their sins and asked for forgiveness. But Proverbs 28:13 tells us: "People who cover over their sins will not prosper. But if they confess and forsake them, they will receive mercy."

Notice that two things are necessary: confessing and forsaking. How can you expect to have victory over guilt if you confess a certain sin and then commit it again? You neglected to *forsake* it.

James 5:16 adds, "Confess your sins to each other and pray for each other so that you may be healed."

"It's not that easy, Steve."

You're right; sometimes it's not. Temptation can be strong, but "remember that the temptations that come into your life are no different from what others experience. And God is faithful. He will keep the temptation from becoming so strong that you can't stand up against it. When you are tempted, he will show you a way out so that you will not give in to it" (1 Corinthians 10:13).

Sometimes we confess too glibly. We rattle off a "forgive me list" to God, whereas the confession would have a far more profound impact upon our soul if we were to confess to the people we've wronged. If you lied about a friend, it is important to confess your sin to God—but a confession to your friend might also impress the destructive nature of gossip and lying upon your soul.

Take care of the past. Silence those accusing voices by confessing and forsaking your sins as they arise. If you have repented of past sins, leave those failures at the cross and do not allow them to haunt you. If you are bitter because others have wronged you, go to them in love and share the burden on your heart. If they ask your forgiveness, give it freely. If they do not acknowledge the hurt, forgive them anyway, and leave the burden behind. Remember, to forgive calls upon your love. To forget calls upon your strength.[11]

What about the guilt that won't go away? If the matter troubling your conscience is not a problem that can be confessed and forsaken, often it is the result of false guilt. If your mother died while you were away from home so you were not able to get to the hospital in time, there is no reason for you to bear guilt. You could not have stopped her death.

If, when you were a child, your parents divorced and you have scarcely seen one of them since that time, do not carry false guilt for their breakup. Children often consider themselves responsible for their parents' divorce, but adults divorce because they decide to. Do not carry false guilt for someone else's actions.

Perhaps you were asked by an aunt to speak to your mother and beg her to reconcile a family breach. You tried, but your mother refused to reconcile with her sister. Listen, friend—there's no need to punish yourself for not accomplishing the impossible. You cannot reconcile two people who are not willing to make things right. If you feel guilty for failing, you are carrying a burden of guilt that has no business being on your shoulders.

Perhaps you are carrying a burden of guilt that was imposed by other people. Many Christians, especially those who were raised in strict homes, feel guilty for playing cards, watching football on Sunday, even dancing with their spouse in the privacy of their own home! My friend, do not let man-made rules and regulations burden you unnecessarily. When some early Christians sought to encumber new converts with the strictures of the law, Paul soundly rebuked them. He wrote: "I know what enthusiasm they have for God, but it is misdirected zeal" (Romans 10:2).

We have to be careful here, because we don't want to excuse or condone sin. When we have a question about righteousness, we must go directly to God's Word and search the Scriptures. How can we stay pure? By obeying the Word of God and following its rules (Psalm 119:9). Some practices are clearly identified as sin.

If we fail to find a specific reference that deals with our question, we should pray and seek the Spirit's guidance. There's no need to carry the weight of other men's convictions unless the Spirit impresses them upon our heart as well.

Finally, know this: There is nothing we have done that is so bad that we can't be forgiven. There is no guilt too deep, no wrong too severe, nothing that can't be forgiven and washed away in the sea of God's forgetfulness. "If we confess our sins to him," the Bible tells us, "he is faithful and just to forgive us and to cleanse us from every wrong" (1 John 1:9). And God says, "I will forgive their wrongdoings, and I will never again remember their sins" (Hebrews 8:12).

Yes, my friend, your present is colored by your past. But you can choose the colors of your future.

COOL YOUR ANGER

The third barrier to obtaining our flashpoint goals is anger. Anger drains our energy and power, diverts our concentration and focus, contaminates our motivation, and eliminates insight.

John Hunter, the British physician responsible for developing surgery in the eighteenth century, suffered from angina brought on by anger. "My life is at the mercy of any scoundrel who chooses to put me in a passion," he declared. His words proved prophetic when, at a meeting of the board of St. George's Hospital in London, he became involved in a heated argument with other board members, walked out of the meeting, and dropped dead in the next room.[12]

Anger is the emotion of our displeasure about something we perceive as evil. Humans are as susceptible to anger as they

175

are to love, and many people are surprised to realize that anger is not always a sin. After all, Jesus, who never sinned, was angry when he threw the money changers out of the temple. So when is anger wrong?

Ephesians 4:26 tells us, "'Don't sin by letting anger gain control over you.' Don't let the sun go down while you are still angry."

Anger can become sin when it is *prolonged*. When we are angry, Scripture tells us, we must settle the matter as soon as possible. Anger suppurates like a boil under the skin, festering and flaming until the initial offense takes on a life of its own. David wrote: "Don't sin by letting anger gain control over you. Think about it overnight and remain silent" (Psalm 4:4).

A good night's sleep and the calm light of another day can help us put things in perspective. The event or action that seemed so terrible the day before can seem smaller and less awful when we have allowed our emotions to settle.

Anger is also sin when it is *meritless*. If you become angry at some imagined or accidental offense, your trigger is too touchy. Life is too short to go around being angry because you've only imagined that someone set out to spite you.

Anger is sin when it is *excessive*. People who overreact make life miserable for themselves and for the people who love them. Family members learn to tiptoe around the person with a short temper, because anything can light the fuse! Such a person, the Bible says, is a fool: "A fool is quick-tempered, but a wise person stays calm when insulted" (Proverbs 12:16).

Dr. Benjamin Carson, director of pediatric neurosurgery at Johns Hopkins Hospital in Baltimore, is known the world over for his surgical skills and his care for his young patients.

But in his early life he had a terrible problem with his temper—until a flashpoint experience changed everything.

Carson's parents divorced when he was eight years old. He says, "I adopted God as my earthly father as well as my Heavenly Father when I was fourteen."[13]

While running with some teenagers from the neighborhood, Carson got into a scuffle with another youth. He drew a knife and stabbed at the other boy, but the blade caught on the boy's belt buckle. That moment—and the realization that only a belt had saved both the other teen's life and his own—was the flashpoint experience Carson needed. He went home and fell to his knees.

"I had tried to stab another teenager, and I recognized that I had a personality defect with my terrible temper. I prayed for three hours and asked the Lord to take that defect away. I had been reading *Psychology Today,* and I knew it was difficult to change a personality defect, but God took it away from me. Since then I've never had a problem with my temper."

If Ben Carson's blade had struck higher—or if he had not conquered his temper and had later engaged in another street fight—it is doubtful he would ever have become the excellent surgeon he is today. And hundreds of patients would have been deprived of his compassionate care.

Anger has the power to short-circuit your flashpoint goals and your plans. Don't let anger destroy your life.

Solomon wrote: "Short-tempered people must pay their own penalty. If you rescue them once, you will have to do it again" (Proverbs 19:19), and "A person without self-control is as defenseless as a city with broken-down walls" (Proverbs 25:28).

You can learn to restrain your anger by cultivating self-control. When you are tempted to become angry, take time for a walk, count to ten, go into a room and close the door. Yell, if you must, but yell at the wall, your pillow, an empty chair. Later, when you are calm, go out and face the problem. Confront the mistake, the error, or the person who insulted you, and speak with patience and honesty.

"My dear brothers and sisters," wrote the apostle James, "be quick to listen, slow to speak, and slow to get angry" (James 1:19).

Edwin Stanton, Abraham Lincoln's secretary of war, experienced frequent difficulty with a general who accused him of favoritism. Stanton complained to President Lincoln, who suggested that he write the officer a sharp letter.

Stanton did and showed the strongly worded note to the president. Lincoln applauded the forceful language of the letter, then asked, "What are you going to do with it?"

Surprised, Stanton replied, "Send it, of course."

Lincoln shook his head. "You don't want to send that letter. Put it in the stove. That's what I do when I have written a letter while I am angry. It's a good letter and you had a good time writing it and feel better. Now burn it, and write another."[14]

Lincoln's advice was Scripture in action. Be angry, but sin not. Retain control of your spirit, and guard your words.

I don't think that anybody has the capacity to anger us like our children. Perhaps it's because we care for them so deeply—when you care to the depths of your soul, there is a fine line between passionate love and passionate anger. If we didn't care, we wouldn't feel anything, but when we care more than anything in the world, fireworks can fly.

One woman told me about her experience with her eighteen-year-old son. "I knew the teen years would be difficult and that my son would begin to pull away from us," she said. "So I expected that he'd want to spend all his time with his friends; I tolerated the closed door and the sometimes surly attitude. But one day while working on my children's computer, I discovered a Web page my son had published. There, in living color for the world to see, my son had written about us, his parents, in obscenity-laced language that left no doubts about his feelings toward his family. He hated us, pure and simple. I read things that felt like a knife through my heart. Honestly, if he had stabbed us in the dead of night, I couldn't have been more surprised or more devastated. His father and I had done all we could to love this kid, raise him in a Christian home, and lead him to the Lord, and now I was reading things that chilled my blood.

"My first reaction was stunned disbelief, but how can you doubt something that's staring you in the face? Then I was hurt, and then I began to become angry. I called my husband in, and together we read the words that had rocked my world. Together we sat in silence and wept, crying out to God for wisdom.

"We didn't know what to do. But something in me wanted to call my son into the room and say, 'So this is what you think of us? Fine. If you hate us so much, take whatever you can carry and leave this house. You are eighteen, and if you don't want us as parents, if you don't agree with our principles or guidelines, you can leave. Go now, and don't even think about coming back.'

"That sounds like an awful thing for a parent to say,

doesn't it? But I'd be less than honest if I said I felt any other way. I'd been hurt so deeply after giving so much that I didn't want to open my heart up to hurt again. Anger was a natural defense mechanism.

"But as I wept and agonized, I realized that every time I sin—every single time—I disappoint my heavenly Father just as my son had disappointed me. And did he ever cast me out? No. He allowed me to feel the consequences of my actions, and I certainly lost fellowship when I turned my back on his guidance, but I never lost my relationship to God.

"In the end, we called our son into our bedroom and told him that we loved him, but we couldn't allow him to continue deceiving us. If he wanted to leave, he could, but he would always be welcome in our home if he was willing to repent and return. 'We will always love you,' we said, 'but we cannot support you while you are treating us with disrespect. You have a choice—stay here or go. But if you go, know that we will always love you and want you as a part of our family.'

"Things didn't improve overnight, but they did improve. My son didn't leave, except when he went to college, and I have to admit there's still an ache in my heart when I think about the horrid things I read on the Web. But my anger is gone . . . because I saw myself in my son. And in dealing with him, I'm trying to model my heavenly Father, who is a far more righteous parent than I could ever be."

Anger is destructive, my friend, and love heals. If you are carrying a burden of anger against someone, it's time to drop that burden at Jesus' feet. "Stop your anger! Turn from your rage!" (Psalm 37:8). Turn to Jesus.

EPILOGUE

THE CHANGE ITSELF IS NOTHING; WHEN WE HAVE MADE IT,

THE NEXT WISH IS TO CHANGE AGAIN.

THE WORLD IS NOT YET EXHAUSTED; LET ME SEE

SOMETHING TOMORROW

WHICH I NEVER SAW BEFORE.   —SAMUEL JOHNSON,
Rasselas, 1759

THE OTHER DAY I was out driving through a residential area when I spied two little girls, probably five or six years old, turning cartwheels on their front lawn. They were cartwheeling in gleeful abandon, their bare feet flying through the air in a blur of smiles and summer dresses.

I don't know how long it has been since you turned a cartwheel, but it has been years for me. I do remember one thing about them: If you stop to think while you're doing it, you won't wheel at all. Instead, you'll end up with one of those awkward hand-hand-swing-your-rear-around movements that always made kids giggle in gym class.

Sometimes goals are like that. After you've decided to move ahead, after the planning and evaluating are done, sometimes the best thing you can do is to start running, lift up your hands, and throw yourself into a cartwheel. (I'm speaking figuratively, of course.) Anything less than complete and total commitment will leave you looking awkward and uncertain.

We've covered a lot of ground in this book. By now you should know *what* a flashpoint experience is (that moment when you realize something that could change your life); *who* can have one (anyone, including you!); *how* to implement the change (through illumination, inspiration, evaluation, motivation, and determination); and *why* you should pursue one (because you might change your own life—and maybe the entire world).

Only one question remains: *When* are you going to take the leap?

There's no time like the present.

A few years ago, I was reading one of the syndicated newspaper advice columns (it was either Dear Abby or Ann Landers, I can't remember which), and one of the letters was from a woman who had come to a flashpoint moment and realized she wanted to go to law school. "But that will take three years!" she wailed. "I'll be forty by the time I finish!"

Abby (or Ann), with her usual wisdom and insight, replied, "And how old will you be in three years if you *don't* go to law school?"

Where will you be in three years if you don't pursue your

flashpoint goals? You'll be a few yards farther down the road, with nothing but ordinary life to show for it. Those who risk nothing, gain nothing.

A wise man once said, "Excellence can be attained if you risk more than others think is safe, care more than others think is wise, dream more than others think is practical, and expect more than others think is possible."[1]

Another man said, "If you play it safe in life, you've decided you don't want to grow anymore."

If God has led you to a flashpoint moment, if he has given you the freedom to pursue a goal, then step out in faith. Faith is the flame that will fire your passion. As encouragement, I can think of no better motivating Scripture passage than the "roll call of faith" found in Hebrews 11:1–12:3:

> WHAT IS FAITH? IT IS THE CONFIDENT ASSURANCE THAT WHAT WE HOPE FOR IS GOING TO HAPPEN. IT IS THE EVIDENCE OF THINGS WE CANNOT YET SEE. . . .
>
> IT WAS BY FAITH THAT NOAH BUILT AN ARK TO SAVE HIS FAMILY FROM THE FLOOD. HE OBEYED GOD, WHO WARNED HIM ABOUT SOMETHING THAT HAD NEVER HAPPENED BEFORE. . . .
>
> IT WAS BY FAITH THAT ABRAHAM OBEYED WHEN GOD CALLED HIM TO LEAVE HOME AND GO TO ANOTHER LAND THAT GOD WOULD GIVE HIM AS HIS INHERITANCE. HE WENT WITHOUT KNOWING WHERE HE WAS GOING. AND EVEN WHEN HE REACHED THE LAND GOD PROMISED HIM, HE LIVED THERE BY FAITH. . . .
>
> IT WAS BY FAITH THAT SARAH TOGETHER WITH ABRAHAM WAS ABLE TO HAVE A CHILD, EVEN THOUGH THEY WERE TOO OLD AND SARAH WAS BARREN. . . .

It was by faith that Abraham offered Isaac as a sacrifice when God was testing him. . . .

It was by faith that Isaac blessed his two sons, Jacob and Esau. He had confidence in what God was going to do in the future.

It was by faith that Jacob, when he was old and dying, blessed each of Joseph's sons and bowed in worship as he leaned on his staff.

And it was by faith that Joseph, when he was about to die, confidently spoke of God's bringing the people of Israel out of Egypt. He was so sure of it that he commanded them to carry his bones with them when they left!

It was by faith that Moses' parents hid him for three months. They saw that God had given them an unusual child, and they were not afraid of what the king might do. . . .

It was by faith that Moses left the land of Egypt. . . .

It was by faith that the people of Israel went right through the Red Sea as though they were on dry ground. . . .

It was by faith that the people of Israel marched around Jericho seven days, and the walls came crashing down.

It was by faith that Rahab the prostitute did not die with all the others in her city who refused to obey God. For she had given a friendly welcome to the spies.

WELL, HOW MUCH MORE DO I NEED TO SAY? IT WOULD TAKE TOO LONG TO RECOUNT THE STORIES OF THE FAITH OF GIDEON, BARAK, SAMSON, JEPHTHAH, DAVID, SAMUEL, AND ALL THE PROPHETS. BY FAITH THESE PEOPLE OVERTHREW KINGDOMS, RULED WITH JUSTICE, AND RECEIVED WHAT GOD HAD PROMISED THEM. . . . THEIR WEAKNESS WAS TURNED TO STRENGTH. . . .

ALL OF THESE PEOPLE WE HAVE MENTIONED RECEIVED GOD'S APPROVAL BECAUSE OF THEIR FAITH, YET NONE OF THEM RECEIVED ALL THAT GOD HAD PROMISED. FOR GOD HAD FAR BETTER THINGS IN MIND FOR US THAT WOULD ALSO BENEFIT THEM, FOR THEY CAN'T RECEIVE THE PRIZE AT THE END OF THE RACE UNTIL WE FINISH THE RACE.

THEREFORE, SINCE WE ARE SURROUNDED BY SUCH A HUGE CROWD OF WITNESSES TO THE LIFE OF FAITH, LET US STRIP OFF EVERY WEIGHT THAT SLOWS US DOWN, ESPECIALLY THE SIN THAT SO EASILY HINDERS OUR PROGRESS. AND LET US RUN WITH ENDURANCE THE RACE THAT GOD HAS SET BEFORE US. WE DO THIS BY KEEPING OUR EYES ON JESUS, ON WHOM OUR FAITH DEPENDS FROM START TO FINISH. HE WAS WILLING TO DIE A SHAMEFUL DEATH ON THE CROSS BECAUSE OF THE JOY HE KNEW WOULD BE HIS AFTERWARD. NOW HE IS SEATED IN THE PLACE OF HIGHEST HONOR BESIDE GOD'S THRONE IN HEAVEN. THINK ABOUT ALL HE ENDURED WHEN SINFUL PEOPLE DID SUCH TERRIBLE THINGS TO HIM, SO THAT YOU DON'T BECOME WEARY AND GIVE UP.

God is faithful to provide, encourage, and equip us for what lies ahead. If God were to add your story to this passage from

Hebrews 11, what would it say? "By faith, [insert your name here] . . . did what?"

What is God calling you to do? And how will you accomplish your dream? Through illumination, inspiration, evaluation, motivation, and determination, to be sure. But most of all, through faith.

A few months ago I received the following letter:

> Dear Stephen:
>
> Hi, my name is Kassie, and I'm in the San Jacinto County Jail. I received your book, *The God of Second Chances*. Your book has shown me so much and opened my eyes to a new world. . . . I am only eighteen, and this is my first time in jail. I chose the wrong path, and now I have chosen the narrow path. I went to church my whole life, and I went the wrong way two years ago. Today I have to pay for it, but I have been given that second chance. . . . God is so faithful, nothing can compare to him!

I have to tell you that the above letter is more than enough to make me feel fulfilled. If Kassie's life was the only life I ever influenced, my effort to write and work would be worth the struggle. Kassie's eyes were opened to a new world. Can you imagine what it must feel like to have your eyes opened while in prison? Just when you discover freedom in Christ, you must come to terms with where your previous choices have brought you. But, as Jesus said, "If the Son sets you free, you will indeed be free" (John 8:36).

Paul wrote: "For you have been called to live in freedom—not freedom to satisfy your sinful nature, but freedom to serve one another in love" (Galatians 5:13).

We are free, not to do as we choose, but to pursue the dreams God places in our heart. He works within us to perform his will, and his will is good and far more than we could ask or think. He has a unique plan for each of us, a plan formed of love and care and compassion. His plan for you will no doubt involve enough trial to bring you to maturity, but he will never abandon you, fail you, or leave you without comfort. God wants to "make you strong and perfect, fully confident of the whole will of God" (Colossians 4:12).

A friend of mine told me about a story she saw on the History Channel about a bridge builder who worked during World War II. This man, whose name has been lost to the ages, was responsible for building bridges and roads along military escape routes.

None of his bridges stand today, and most of his roads have either vanished beneath modern highways or gone back to forest vegetation. A twenty-first century European might think that this anonymous man had accomplished little in his lifetime.

But his roads and bridges were the sole means of escape for thousands who fled the bombings in Europe. Without his work, untold hundreds of men, women, and children would have perished in the woods or been left behind during the Nazi invasions. If they had died, their future children and their children's children would never have been born. But they escaped to safety . . . because one man was called to do a job, and he did his work well.[2]

I don't know what God is calling you to do. He may be

urging you to do something as personal as improve your health. Perhaps he is leading you to start a business or begin a ministry. Maybe it's time to get into the workforce or out of the workforce; to start painting or writing or composing music. If you have children, he certainly wants you to train them in righteousness.

Start right where you are—but don't rule out the possibility that God is directing you to something big that will have a profound and far-reaching effect on you, your family, and your community.

Take the vision God has given you and enter the race. It may be that in one hundred years no one will be able to see the results of your labor. Or it may be that your work will be the foundation for other effective works done in Christ's name.

No godly work is done in vain. The repercussions are eternal, and so are the blessings.

So—what will you do? Will you have to wait until all your options are exhausted before you open your heart to a flashpoint moment? Will you have to reach the bottom before you're willing to look up to the God who created you and loves you?

I hope not. In this very moment you have an opportunity to say yes to the yearning God has placed in your heart. Don't neglect the opportunity. Recognize what you need to change, and accept the vision God has given you. If an eighteen-year-old prisoner like Kassie can turn her life around while she's in jail, certainly you, with all your freedom and opportunity, can do the same. The time for your flashpoint is *now*.

ENDNOTES

CHAPTER ONE: FINDING YOUR FLASHPOINT

1. Michael Ryan, "The World Is Full of Children to Love," *Parade*, 15 July 2001, 4–6.
2. Walt Disney quoted on www.quoteland.com

CHAPTER TWO: SPIRITUAL FLASHPOINTS

1. C. S. Lewis, *The Silver Chair* (New York: HarperTrophy, 1981), 20–21.
2. My thanks to novelist Randy Alcorn for suggesting these two Lewis passages.
3. C. S. Lewis, *The Lion, the Witch, and the Wardrobe* (New York: HarperTrophy, 1978), 86.
4. Stephen Arterburn and Fred Stoeker, *Every Man's Battle* (Colorado Springs: WaterBrook, 2000).

CHAPTER THREE: FINANCIAL FLASHPOINTS

1. Randy Alcorn, *Money, Possessions, and Eternity* (Wheaton, Ill.: Tyndale House Publishers, 1989), 17.
2. C. S. Lewis quoted in Randy Alcorn's *Money, Possessions, and Eternity* (Wheaton, Ill.: Tyndale House Publishers, 1989), 15.
3. Craig Wilson, "Life's Simplest Luxuries Dwarf All That 'Stuff,'" *USA Today*, 3 January 2001.
4. Ibid.

5. Randy Alcorn, *The Treasure Principle* (Sisters, Oreg.: Multnomah Publishers, 2001), 18–19.
6. John Gray, "How We Can Create Miracles, Too," *Bottom Line Personal*, 15 February 2001, 2.
7. Edward Wong, "Hearing God's Call As Illness Strikes," *New York Times*, 28 March 2001.

CHAPTER FOUR: PHYSICAL FLASHPOINTS
1. John Davenport, "So, How's Your Health?" *Newsweek*, 2 August 1999, 48.
2. Ibid.
3. Ibid.
4. Carol Humphreys, "Cancer Survivor Is Now Dedicated to Educating Others," *Orange County Register*, 6 November 2000.
5. Elizabeth Cohen, "Federal Study of Diets Concludes: Eat Less," CNN.com Food Central (10 January 2001).
6. Ibid.
7. Web sites: www.weight.addr.com/BMI.html *or* sleephelpusa.com/bmi-start.phtml
8. C. S. Lewis quoted in Mark Buchanan, *Your God Is Too Safe* (Sisters, Oreg.: Multnomah Publishers, 2001), 191.
9. Buchanan, *Your God Is Too Safe*, 192.

CHAPTER FIVE: CAREER FLASHPOINTS
1. Joy Marple, ed., *Prescription for Life* (Grand Rapids, Mich.: Zondervan Publishing House, 1997), 50.
2. Alecia Swasy, "A Practical Guide to Starting Over," *New York Times*, 11 March 2001.
3. Phil Patton, "People Who Made a Difference," *Reader's Digest*, April 1998, 105–108.
4. Elaine St. James, "New Year's Resolutions," *Bottom Line Personal*, 1 January 2001, 8.
5. Ibid.
6. Robert Reich, "Your Job Is Change," *Fast Company*, October 2000, 158.
7. Martin Arnold, "Making Books," *New York Times*, 22 March 2001.
8. Clifton Fadiman, *The Little, Brown Book of Anecdotes* (Boston: Little, Brown and Company, 1985), 209.
9. Jane Ciabattari, "All You Have to Do Is Try," *Parade*, 27 May 2001, 9.
10. Ann Oldenburg, "Dr. Phil's Advice: Wake Up!" *USA Today*, 8 May 2001.
11. Margo Jefferson, "Worth More Than It Costs," *New York Times Book Review*, 1 April 2001, 12.
12. Jim Hopkins, "Single Mom Beats Cancer, Sexism on Way to Success," *USA Today*, 19 January 2001.

13. George Anders, "Are You on the Right Track?" *Fast Company,* December 2000, 156.

CHAPTER SIX: LIFESTYLE FLASHPOINTS

1. William R. Mattox Jr., "Outsiders Step Forward to Deter Divorce," *USA Today,* 14 February 2001.
2. Jane Ciabattari, "Now I'm a Giver instead of a Taker," *Parade,* 22 April 2001, 4–5.
3. Susan Vaughn, "Looking on the Lighter Side of 'The Change,'" *Los Angeles Times,* 20 December 2000.
4. Jodi Wilgoren, "Five Determined Students, Five Unusual Routes to a College Degree," *New York Times,* 27 May 2001.
5. Dotson Rader, "He's Lived the Life He Sings," *Parade,* 20 December 2000, 7.
6. Candi Cushman, "Changed Hearts," *World,* 21 April 2001, 19–21.
7. Lori Basheda, "A Down Payment on Hope," *Orange County Register,* 28 May 2001.
8. Daniel De Vise, "Boy's Disappearance in '81 Changed Nation," *Tampa Tribune,* 27 July 2001.

CHAPTER SEVEN: ARE YOU READY FOR A FLASHPOINT?

1. Joy Marple, ed., *Prescription for Life* (Grand Rapids, Mich.: Zondervan Publishing House, 1997), 104.
2. Edwin Arlington Robinson, "Richard Cory," in *Representative Poetry On-Line,* ed. I. Lancanshire (Univ. of Toronto Lib.: Web Development Group, Inf. Tech. Services).
3. Ted Turner quoted in *The New York Public Library Book of Twentieth Century American Quotations,* ed. Stephen Donadio et al. (New York: Warner Books, 1992), 272.
4. Alexander Haig quoted in *The New York Public Library Book of Twentieth Century American Quotations,* 139.
5. John Corry quoted in *The New York Public Library Book of Twentieth Century American Quotations,* 13.
6. Hugh Leonard quoted in *The Oxford Dictionary of Quotations* (New York: Oxford University Press, 1999), 464.
7. Louis R. Harlan, ed.; John W. Blassingame, asst. ed., *The Autobiographical Writings,* vol. 1 of *The Booker T. Washington Papers* (Urbana and Chicago: University of Illinois Press, 1972), 303.
8. George Herbert quoted in "Reflections," compiled by Richard Kauffman, *Christianity Today,* 8 January 2001, 82.
9. David Abrahamsen quoted in *The New York Public Library Book of Twentieth Century American Quotations,* 418.

CHAPTER EIGHT: CAPTURING THE SPARK

1. Derric Johnson, *Excellence Is Never an Accident* (Tulsa: Trade Life Books, 1997), 11.
2. Elizabeth Barrett Browning, *Aurora Leigh,* Book VII (London: J. Miller, 1864).
3. Mark Buchanan, *Your God Is Too Safe* (Sisters, Oreg.: Multnomah Publishers, 2001), 149–50.
4. Natashia Gregoire, "Owner Takes Plunge with All Her Soaps," *Tampa Tribune,* 26 July 2001.
5. Johnson, *Excellence Is Never an Accident,* 117.
6. Ibid., 132.
7. Tad Szulc, "Enjoy Life, Day by Day," *Parade,* 25 March 2001, 4–5.
8. John Graham, "You Can!!! You Can!!!" *Bottom Line Personal,* 15 January 2001, 13.
9. Ibid.
10. Booker T. Washington, *Up from Slavery, An Autobiography* (New York: Doubleday, Page & Co., 1901), 234.

CHAPTER NINE: GIVING WINGS TO YOUR DREAMS

1. Daniel Levine, "My First Job," *Reader's Digest,* March 2001, 103.
2. Frank Witsil, "King of the Road," *Tampa Tribune,* 30 July 2001.
3. Richard Allestree, *The Government of the Tongue,* quoted in *Discipleship Journal* 122 (March/April 2001): 106.
4. Clifton Fadiman, ed., *The Little, Brown Book of Anecdotes* (Boston: Little, Brown and Company, 1985), 362.
5. Levine, "My First Job," 99.
6. Adapted from "Resilience Rules" by Andrew Shatte, *Fast Company,* April 2001, 155.
7. Derric Johnson, *Excellence Is Never an Accident* (Tulsa: Trade Life Books, 1997), 67.
8. Ibid., 123.
9. Ruth La Ferla, "Sleep, the Final Luxury," *New York Times,* 11 December 2000.
10. Michele Bearden, "Midlife Ministers," *Tampa Tribune,* 26 July 2001.

CHAPTER TEN: FLASHPOINT BARRIERS

1. Clifton Fadiman, ed., *The Little, Brown Book of Anecdotes* (Boston: Little, Brown and Company, 1985), 422.
2. Norman Vincent Peale quoted in *The New York Public Library Book of Twentieth Century American Quotations,* ed. Stephen Donadio et al. (New York: Warner Books, 1992), 252.
3. Andrea Hughie, "A Holiday Toy That's Intended to Be Dubious," *New York Times,* 5 December 2000.
4. Fadiman, *Book of Anecdotes,* 414.

5. Derric Johnson, *Excellence Is Never an Accident* (Tulsa: Trade Life Books, 1997), 101.

6. Fadiman, *Book of Anecdotes,* 210.

7. Jeffrey Kluger, "Phobias: Fear Not! For Millions of Sufferers, Science Is Offering New Treatments—and New Hope," *Time,* 2 April 2001, 54, 62.

8. Ibid., 62.

9. Jean Toomer quoted in *The New York Public Library Book of Twentieth Century American Quotations,* 252.

10. Stanley Hauerwas quoted in "Reflections," compiled by Richard Kauffman, *Christianity Today,* 8 January 2001, 82.

11. Johnson, *Excellence Is Never an Accident,* 41.

12. Fadiman, *Book of Anecdotes,* 294.

13. Angela Elwell Hunt, "Thinking Big, Flying High," *The Lookout,* 23 September 1990, 4.

14. Fadiman, *Book of Anecdotes,* 360.

EPILOGUE

1. Derric Johnson, *Excellence Is Never an Accident* (Tulsa: Trade Life Books, 1997), 55.

2. With thanks to author Sandra Byrd, who provided this story.

STEPHEN ARTERBURN is the creator of Women of Faith conferences, the largest traveling conference in the United States, and New Life Clinics, the world's largest provider of Christian counseling. You can hear him weekdays on the live call-in radio program *New Life Live* on a Christian radio station in your area. He is the editor of *The Life Recovery Bible,* the author of more than forty books, and has received a Gold Medallion award. He lives with his amazing wife, their soccer-playing daughter, and three dogs in Laguna Beach, California. Steve's e-mail address is SArterburn@newlife.com

Christy-award winning author ANGELA HUNT is the author of more than eighty books, including the best-selling *Tale of Three Trees, The Note,* and *The Immortal.* She lives with her husband and two teenagers in Florida.